Hill Walkers
Wicklow

Layout, Sketch Maps: Shanksmare Publications
Sketches: Ruth Herman
Typesetting by: Hot Pixels Design
Printed by: Colour Books Ltd, Dublin 13
Published by: Shanksmare Publications, 41 Meadow Grove, Dublin 16

ISBN 0 9514547 5 7

Front Cover: Looking North from Maulin
Back Cover: Glenmalure and Clohernagh

The Author

David Herman has many years' experience exploring the mountains of Ireland and further afield. As well as two guides describing the mountains of Ireland in general, he has written detailed guides to various regions of the country.

Other books written by the author under the Shanksmare imprint are: *Hill Walkers Kerry* (1997), *Hill Walkers Connemara and Mayo* (1996), *Hill Walkers Donegal* (1995), *Hill Strollers Wicklow* (1994) and *North Leitrim Glens* (1993). Other books by the author include *Great Walks Ireland* (Ward Lock, 1991), *Walker's Companion* (Ward Lock, 1995), *Walking Ireland's Mountains* (Appletree, 1994). He is co-author of *Walk Guide East of Ireland* (Gill and Macmillan, 1996).

Acknowledgements

I've said it many times before and I'll probably say it again: I would like to thank my dear wife Máirín, who walked all these routes with me and without whose help, both on the mountains and at home, this book or any other in the series, would not have been written.

Hill Walkers Wicklow

29 One-Day Walking Routes in the Mountains near Dublin

David Herman

SHANKSMARE PUBLICATIONS

The lake is bounded on three Sides by vaft high and almoft inacceffible Mountains, that on the weft Side is of prodigeous Height. Through the middle Part there gently glides a fmart River, from one Rock to another....

A description of Glendalough, taken from *'A New Geography of Ireland'* (1752), by James Eyre Weeks

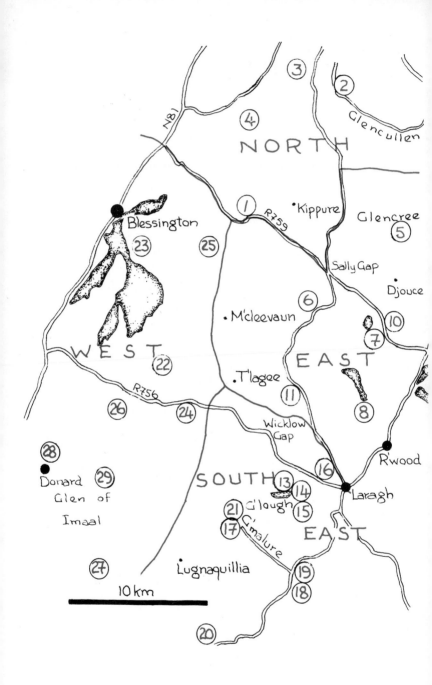

CONTENTS

Introduction to the 1997 Edition p6; A Quick Look Around p6; How to Use this Book p7; Accessing the Mountains from Dublin p8; Maps p9; Safety p10; What to Carry with You p11; A Few Route Selections p11; Planning Your Own Routes p11; The Country Code p12; You, Landowners and the Law p12, They're Your Mountains, Too! p13; Useful Contacts p13.

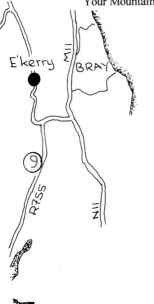

    *   Routes with Major Variations

INTRODUCTION TO THE 1997 EDITION

For the present edition I have taken the opportunity to vary the routes as much as possible from those in the previous edition which appeared in 1993. The format has been modified so that there is now a uniform series of books covering some of the mountain areas of Ireland, a series which, I hope, will eventually cover all the main mountain areas.

The most important development that has occurred in the Wicklow mountains since 1993, apart from the continuing increase in the numbers walking in the mountain areas and the expansion of modern mapping to the entire range, the latter dealt with below, has been the further expansion of the Wicklow Mountains National Park, so that it now covers two-thirds of its target area. This is a most welcome development, ensuring as it does that the Wicklow mountains, a vital natural resource, will be conserved for future generations. It behoves all of us who walk in and cherish these mountains to help the Park authorities in any way we can.

A QUICK LOOK AROUND

Dubliners are lucky to have on their doorsteps the largest area of upland in Ireland, an area encompassing some fine peaks, beautiful mountain valleys cradling lovely lakes and vast (maybe too vast) areas of moorland.

Let's first look briefly at the whole of the mountain area in outline, describing briefly the four regions into which the book is divided. The exact boundaries of these regions are shown on the key map (pages 4-5).

The North (routes 1-4), the area nearest Dublin, is greatly influenced by the city itself. This proximity has some advantages but more disadvantages. The main advantage is that the area is easy to access, with public transport reaching some fairly good mountain areas. The main disadvantage stems from this proximity: masts of all types, litter and overcrowded and eroded paths and tracks. The terrain itself consists mostly of gently rounded peaks and shoulders, the city and coastline in view from the north-east corner, and the area further west offering a more remote ambience.

The East (routes 5-11) encompasses some of the most attractive scenery in Wicklow, though unfortunately - and indeed consequently - there are a few badly eroded areas. The area round two large mountain lakes, Tay and Dan (routes 7, 8), which are partly surrounded by fine peaks, offers particularly memorable walking. Further west beyond the Military Road the spine of the range runs through the second and third highest peaks in the Wicklow mountains, Mullaghcleevaun (849m) and Tonelagee (817m), the latter an especially fine mountain (routes 11, 16, 25).

The South-East (routes 12-21) is focused around two well-known and scenic valleys. Glendalough is a glacial valley with strong historical associations and is almost surrounded by distinctive peaks (routes 13-15). It is a deservedly popular centre for walking and has a modest though invaluable bus service from Dublin. Further south is Glenmalure, another good centre for walking (routes 17-19). Overlooking Glenmalure is the Lugnaquillia massif, culminating in Lugnaquillia itself (925m). This is a high-level area with some lovely peaks, mountain valleys, cliffs and corries (routes 17, 20, 29). There is a brief guide to accessing the Lugnaquillia massif on page 71.

The West (routes 21-29) is dominated on the north by the large expanse of Pollaphuca Reservoir, a pleasant body of water which enhances the views from the otherwise none too inspiring peaks around it (routes 22, 24-26, 28). Directly south of the R756 road (routes 24, 26, 28) is some of the most desolate country in Wicklow (this is not necessarily a condemnation!). Further south lies the almost circular basin of the Glen of Imaal (routes 27-29), which is backed on the north by some good, though rounded peaks and on the east by the impressive Lugnaquillia massif (discussed above). South of the Glen the mountain country is diversified by agricultural land and some forestry (route 27).

HOW TO USE THIS BOOK

First of all, it is only fair to say that a map must be used with this book. More about suitable maps is given below and in each route description.

I have tried to cover all the best and most characteristic of the mountain areas of counties Wicklow and Dublin - of course the best are not necessarily the most characteristic. In doing so, I have not described every area covered by every route in superlative terms. All the routes chosen have some favourable characteristics and some, and only some, have unfavourable ones. All these judgements are only my evaluation, and you might well have quite different verdicts.

The Sketch Maps: These accompany all the route descriptions and are on the same scale as the best of the OS maps ie 1:50 000 or 2cm to 1km. Their aim is to emphasise what is *not* on the Ordnance Survey (OS) maps eg cliffs and areas of peat hags. Features which are important for navigation and/or reassurance points are shown in red. North is always to the top of the page. The symbols are explained on the inside back cover.

Walking Time: This is based on 4km/hr on the flat and a climbing rate of 500m/hr, so that a walk of 4km with a climb of 250m should take 1½ hours. This is a fairly leisurely pace and if you are reasonably fit you should have no difficulty in keeping to it. The time is adjusted for difficult conditions (eg high vegetation, steep descents) or good (eg clear tracks) and in these instances the adjustment is noted at the appropriate point in the text.

Metric versus Imperial: Metric units are used throughout - if you simply can't think metric you can use the tables on the inside back cover. The one occasion where imperial units are used is where cars are involved, as they are usually equipped with milometers.

Grid References: These are the four or six digit numbers, preceded by the letters 'GR' which appear in this book after some locations, particularly the start of routes. The figure uniquely identifies the location on most maps. The system is explained on all OS maps.

Warning: Things change, even the 'eternal hills'. Of all the mountain ranges in Ireland, Wicklow is probably the one subject to most change. New forest tracks are constructed, there are many areas of fast-growing trees, houses are built across paths and areas which were accessible turn overnight into areas with lines of intimidating fences. Please bear in mind that if the route description does not make sense it is not (necessarily) the author's fault. It could be that there is a new feature in the landscape or that a feature that I describe has disappeared. For the record, with only a few minor exceptions, every section of every route was walked not earlier than spring 1996.

ACCESSING THE MOUNTAINS FROM DUBLIN

I must first apologise for assuming that you will always travel from Dublin to the mountains. However, most hill walkers in these mountains do come from Dublin and it is the one large centre from which all parts of the mountains are best accessed.

By Car

Getting to the mountains from Dublin is not easy because of the complexity of the road network and inadequate sign-posting. The method used here is to use 'jumping-off' points. For each route first drive from Dublin to the appropriate jumping-off point (indicated in *italics* in the paragraph 'Getting There' in the route description). From there drive to the starting point as indicated in the same paragraph.

Here are the jumping-off points (the figures in brackets given after each represents miles from central Dublin):

Blessington (18): Drive through Harold's Cross, Terenure and Templeogue following signs for the N81.

Donard (31) (GR 9397): Follow signs for the N81, turning left at the 'Old Tollhouse', about 11 miles south of Blessington.

Drumgoff crossroads (Glenmalure) (36) (GR 1090): Drive to *Laragh* (see below), continue on the R755 for about 1 mile. Fork right (signed 'Glenmalure') for Drumgoff crossroads, which is about 4½ miles further on.

Enniskerry (13): Follow signs for Ranelagh and Dundrum, then continue straight ahead.

Glenasmole (9) (GR 0922): Follow signs for the N81 (see *Blessington* above) to turn left at the roundabout which leads onto the M50. (Note: there may be alterations to the road network here in the not too distant future.) Turn right at the nearby tee onto the R114 and continue straight ahead for 3.7 miles, turning left here into Glenasmole.

Glendalough (31), *Laragh* (30): Follow signs for the M11/N11 initially through Leeson Street and Donnybrook. Turn right onto the R755 at Kilmacanoge.

Lackan (22) (GR 0111): Follow signs for the N81 to *Blessington*, turn left after Downshire Hotel, turn right shortly over the reservoir, turn right immediately at the tee, continue on the main road to the village.

Rockbrook (6) (GR 1324): Follow signs for Rathfarnham, pass Rathfarnham Castle (on left), turn right shortly after at the Yellow House pub (on right). Continue straight ahead for about 2½ miles to the village.

Roundwood (26) (GR 1903): Follow signs for the M11/N11 initially through Leeson Street and Donnybrook; turn right onto the R755 at Kilmacanoge.

Sally Gap (17) (GR 1311), *Military Road*: Drive initially through Harold's Cross and Terenure following signs for Rathfarnham, pass Rathfarnham Castle (on left), turn right shortly after at the Yellow House pub (on right). Turn right onto Scholarstown Road 1.2 miles from the pub and second left almost immediately onto Stocking Lane and continue straight ahead.

A Word of Caution to Travellers by Car: There have been many thefts in recent years from cars parked in mountain locations. It is therefore advisable never to leave valuables in unattended cars. Do not leave a note visible in your car indicating when you intend to arrive back.

By Bus

The following Dublin Bus services (☎ 01-873 4222) may be useful.

For the north-west corner of the mountains note the services 47 (Tibradden (GR 149253), infrequent), 47A (Rockbrook (GR 137247), moderately frequent), 47B (Grange Road (GR 160257), moderately frequent), 203 (Bohernabreena (GR 096245), frequent).

For Barnacullia (GR 1823), Glencullen (GR 1820), note the 44B service (infrequent).

For the north-east corner note the services 44 (Enniskerry, frequent), and the Shop River variation of the 85 which travels 2.5km west of Enniskerry (moderately frequent).

For the west (N81) note the 65 to Blessington (frequent), Ballymore Eustace, Ballyknockan and Donard (all very infrequent).

There is a very useful service along the east of the range terminating in Glendalough. This is the St Kevin's Bus (☎ 01-281 8119) which runs from St Stephen's Green in Dublin through Kilmacanoge, Roundwood and Laragh to Glendalough. The service is fairly infrequent.

Reid's Buses (☎ 0404-67671) runs a regular service between Wicklow town and Glendalough.

There are two Irish Bus / Bus Eireann local services (ie buses which stop anywhere as long as it is safe to do so) which might be useful for hill walkers. They are bus timetable 132 (very infrequent) which runs from Dublin along the N81 on the west of the range with a useful stop at Annalecky Cross (GR 9199) near Donard, and timetable 133 (frequent) which runs along the N11 (with diversions to villages) on the east of the range.

There is only one Irish Bus / Bus Eireann express (ie limited stop) service which might be useful for hill walkers. It is given on bus timetable 5 with variations which traverse each side of the mountains from Dublin. That on the west stops at Blessington (pick-up only) and at Annalecky Cross. That on the east stops at Bray and Ashford (GR 2797).

MAPS

The whole of the mountain area is adequately covered by the OS Discovery Series on a scale of 1:50 000 with 10m contour interval. Sheet 50 covers roughly the mountains near Dublin, sheet 56 the bulk of the mountain area and is thus the one map you *must* have and sheet 62 the south. There is no overlap between sheets, so both text and sketch maps given in this book give compass bearings to cover the more awkward transitions between sheets.

Since this series will be used by most hill walkers it is worthwhile considering some of its limitations:

- Cliffs are not depicted explicitly on the map, so you must judge their presence by the convergence of contour lines.
- Forest tracks are badly depicted, with many clear tracks omitted. Others are shown where they do not exist. 'Forest tracks' which run up hill and down dale regardless of the terrain are generally firebreaks. The extent of forestry planting has generally been exaggerated.
- The route of the Wicklow Way is badly shown.
- Footpaths and footbridges are generally omitted.
- Some streams in upland areas are depicted by formidably thick lines; nevertheless you can assume that they are normally fordable (the route

descriptions in this book will alert you to streams which are difficult to ford). The courses of other streams are totally obliterated by the National Park boundary line.

The National Parks and Wildlife Service has published a map of the Glendalough area on a scale of 1:25 000 with a 15m contour interval. It covers a small but popular area and is particularly good in its depiction of tracks and paths. It may be obtained at the Visitor Centre in Glendalough.

A strip map on a scale of 1:50 000 covering the route of the Wicklow Way has been published by EastWest Mapping (☎ 054-77835). It is useful for the limited area on the east of the range that it covers because it shows forest tracks and paths correctly, as noted above a major failing with OS maps.

Lastly, there is the 1:126 720 (half-inch to the mile) OS sheet 16, which covers almost the entire mountain area and much more besides. Its scale is far too small and it is out of date and therefore of little use except for giving an overall view of the mountain area and its environs.

The features of the sketch maps given in this book are explained above. They not only show the route but also indicate features not shown on the OS maps.

SAFETY

Before you start out

It is essential to leave your intended route with someone; to have a map and compass and to know how to use them; to wear proper walking boots and carry raingear. It's advisable that at least three walk together. Get a weather forecast by ringing 1550 123 814.

On the Walk

Do not press on regardless in the face of worsening weather or falling night. Remember that the major factor by far affecting route finding in the mountains is visibility. Cloud and fog make all the difference to navigation. As well as the obvious lack of visibility they are disorienting and distorting, so that what is in reality a minor hill near at hand will appear through cloud like a major mountain much further away.

In such inauspicious conditions, try to find out exactly where you are before visibility fails. Pay careful attention to your route and time your progress using Naismith's Rule (and if you don't know what the Rule is, learn it before you venture forth).

If You Get Lost

First, think. A few minutes thought may save hours of blundering around in the dark or in cloud. You must have some idea of where you are. In the Wicklow mountains, where there is much gently shelving terrain the direction of slope might provide a clue. Similarly, a stream's direction might be some use. It might be worthwhile to climb to the nearest top, identify it and start again if it would not be too tiring and demoralising. If you can find one of the navigationally important landmarks marked in this book, it should be a great help.

If darkness is descending it is probably better to face a long road walk (you might get a lift) rather than take a 'short cut' across the hills. Don't plunge into a forestry plantation unless you are absolutely sure that you can emerge at the other side. You may make some progress at first and then find your way completely blocked by impenetrable closely spaced trees - and totally disoriented to cap it all.

WHAT TO CARRY WITH YOU

If you were to carry all the safety equipment that some experts tell you to carry, you would be so weighed down that you wouldn't be able to walk. The most important item to get right are boots, as mentioned above. Apart from that there are only a few things that you really must carry. These include food and a flask with a hot liquid, a whistle and a map and compass. Unless the day looks uncommonly settled and likely to remain so, you should take a waterproof. Lastly, you need a rucksack to put everything else in. Anything else is optional or depends mainly on the weather and the route.

A FEW ROUTE SELECTIONS

If you have limited time in Wicklow and want to get some idea of the flavour of the mountains as well as walking some of the best routes you might like to consider the following selection:

- Route 3, an area close to Dublin which avoids most of the degradation associated with the city's proximity
- Route 7, an easy route in one of the loveliest areas in the mountains
- Route 14, a lovely circuit in Wicklow's favourite walking area
- Route 17, probably the most dramatic approach to Wicklow's highest peak.
- Route 26, Wicklow at its bleakest, yet a satisfying circuit.

PLANNING YOUR OWN ROUTES

The Wicklow mountains constitute the largest area of uplands in Ireland, much of it a wilderness but, by the standard of Irish mountains (note qualification!) without many dangerous areas. They therefore offer unrivalled scope for devising your own routes.

You will note from some of the route descriptions that information is given about the ease with which that particular route may be varied. In general it is easier to vary routes where there are no narrow ridges and cliffs, as is the case in much of Wicklow, and where there has been little forestry planting, as is not the case in much of Wicklow. Unless you know what you are doing it is advisable, if you want to walk anywhere near farmed areas, to start routes at points mentioned in this book; landowners are understandably sensitive about trespassers and the possible damage that uninvited 'guests' can cause.

THE COUNTRY CODE

It is surely not necessary to spell out the whole of the Country Code in detail, as it is just ordinary good manners adapted to the outdoors. Instead let's concentrate on a few of the possibly less obvious points.

- Dogs are a menace in the mountains, as they are in any sheep-rearing area. If you must take one, keep it on a lead for the entire walk.
- If you have to climb a closed gate do at the hinged end where you will cause less damage.
- Path erosion is an ever-increasing eyesore. Don't widen paths by walking on their edges. Don't walk straight up or down hills if there is a zig-zag path. There a few places in this book where I have avoided the 'obvious' path because it is eroded. Take especial care in soft, boggy country as it is particularly fragile.
- Don't climb fences unless there is simply no alternative. If you do, don't stand on the fence wires. They may look the same afterwards but will have been irretrievably damaged.
- Don't litter. Don't leave any, even biodegradable. Do you know how long it takes an orange peel to degrade? Think how unsightly it looks in the meantime. You might even consider taking away other people's litter. This might seem a pretty bizarre idea but it won't take much effort and litter cannot remove itself.
- Car parking. On Sundays many mountain carparks are clogged with cars. Try to minimise over-crowding by sharing cars. Do not park along narrow roads, at driveways or gates or where your car will cause an obstruction to others.

YOU, LANDOWNERS AND THE LAW

The only areas where the walker has right of way are in the National Park, on the Wicklow Way and in certain designated forest areas. In nearly all other areas the walker is there without the permission of the landowner, and therefore should leave if told to do so.

The Occupiers' Liability Act 1995 has cleared up the matter of compensation if an accident occurs on a landowner's land. The walker is in the same legal category as a trespasser and the onus of responsibility for the walker's safety now rests on him/her - as of course it should - and not on the landowner, as the law may have been interpretable up to this. In theory at least this should make landowners a little more tolerant of walkers.

However you should try to avoid the following more difficult circumstances, any of which makes it more likely that you will clash with a local landowner:

- Being near homesteads or in enclosed fields, crossing fences, walls or gates.
- Walking in the lower hills near Dublin. Farmers in this area have suffered serious vandalism from yobbos and are understandably on short fuses.
- Being members of a large party.
- Having a dog, especially if unleashed.
- Generally behaving in an inconsiderate manner.

I have tried to steer you away from areas of conflict that I know about but it is impossible to forecast where trouble might flare in the future. If you are asked to leave an area do so without arguing, unless of course there are serious safety implications.

THEY'RE YOUR MOUNTAINS, TOO!

Ireland is a country with a 'healthy disregard' for the law, and no wonder, since the law in too many instances is only for show and not for enforcement. The end result of all this as far as the environment is concerned is littering, dumping, car wrecks, 'temporary dwellings' that moulder away for decades, and all the rest which are obvious to anyone who wants to see.

I wish there were a simple solution to all this, but there isn't. The best you can do is to obey the law yourself and join one of the voluntary organisations which care about the environment. If you are in a walking club help its conservation group or suggest that one be formed if there isn't one.

The Two-Storey House at the Copse (Routes 7, 8)

USEFUL CONTACTS

Wicklow County Tourism, St Manntan's House, Kilmantin Hill, Wicklow town. ☎ 0404-66058.
Irish Youth Hostel Association / An Oige, 61 Mountjoy Street, Dublin 7. ☎ 01-830 4555.
Dublin Bus: for passenger information phone ☎ 01-873 4222.
Irish Bus / Bus Eireann: for passenger information ☎ 01-836 6111.
Mountaineering Council of Ireland, House of Sport, Longmile Road, Dublin 12. ☎ 01-450 1633.
Mountain Rescue ☎ 999.
St Kevin's Bus Service, Roundwood, County Wicklow. ☎ 01-281 8119.
Ordnance Survey, Phoenix Park, Dublin 8. ☎ 01-820 6100.

13

THE NORTH
ROUTE 1: KIPPURE AND THE UPPER LIFFEY VALLEY

Lots of boggy ground on a pleasant but far from spectacular route high on the broad ridge between Seefingan and Kippure, with good views in some directions but also much evidence of environmental damage. The walk ends with an easy stretch partly along the banks of the infant River Liffey.

Getting There: Drive towards *Blessington* turning left onto the R759 just past the village of Brittas. Follow signs for Sally Gap for 5.7 miles, parking here in

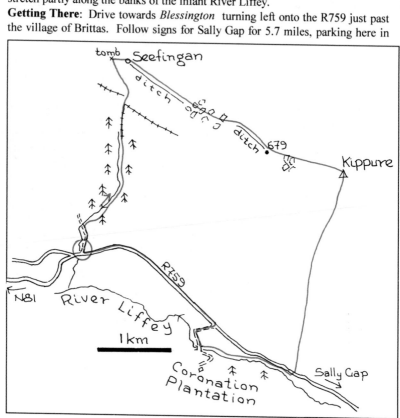

the inconspicuous carpark on the left (GR 079144). It may be more convenient to come from the *Sally Gap* direction. In this case park on the rough ground on the left just after a prominent bridge (at GR 109127) 1.7 miles north-west of Sally Gap and start the walk from there.

Walking Time: 5 hours (distance 13km, climb 560m) including 0.5 hours for difficult underfoot conditions.

Difficulties: Fairly easy navigationally, and even if you get lost there is always the lifeline of the R759 close at hand. Otherwise only lots of bog to worry about.

Map: Sheet 56.

Route: From the carpark take the track for a few minutes and where it enticingly crosses Athdown Brook on the left, do not follow it. Instead keep to the muddy track on the bank you are on and where it expires in forest, walk onward keeping the Brook within reach on the left. Don't stick rigidly to it, because with difficult ground underfoot you may prefer to cross the fence close on the right, and walk upward over somewhat easier ground.

However you manage it you will shortly emerge onto an intermittent path, mature forest on the other side of the Brook, young forest on its near side. At length you will leave both Brook and forest behind, and at a fence running along the south side of the Seefingan to Kippure ridge, take a bearing of about 330° compass for the great megalithic tomb just to the west of the top of Seefingan.

From the tomb walk 200m east to the summit (a notional one) and then follow a ditch south-east along the county boundary. As it approaches a horrible area of peat hags set in an expanse of flat, black mud just to the south-east of pt 657m the ditch supinely disappears. You, however must carry on across this area heading for, and climbing pt 679m, where on easier ground the ditch re-appears. All along here the views, especially to the south are good, with Mullaghcleevaun particularly evident. However most of your attention will probably downward as you navigate a way through the mud.

Point 679m hasn't even a cairn. It does however provide a grandstand view of Kippure, topped by an enormous TV mast, whose near side is a swirl of peat hags with a few improbable grassy stretches reaching towards the summit. So from pt 679m it is a simple matter to drop slightly into the col facing Kippure and then climb through one of these grassy stretches to the nearby summit.

Kippure (757m, 3 hours) is the highest point in county Dublin and commands fairly good views, though otherwise it hasn't a lot to recommend it, as it is a rounded summit whose few natural charms are negated by its burden of the TV mast (masts at the time of writing) and ancillary buildings.

From the summit head south with a touch of west towards the R759, crossing a sturdy fence on the way (a stile may be in place by the time you walk the route) and then descend into high heather. As you advance, head towards the few scattered pines forming the eastern corner of the Coronation Plantation, cross the road and turn right onto the rough path along the stream (it's the infant Liffey).

This is a nice, peaceful stretch: the river gurgling in its rocky bed on the left and the old, dark pines of the Plantation standing out against the almost yellow grasses of the bogland. Walk downstream to a bridge over the river, serving a house set among the trees. Don't cross it: instead take the track up to the nearby road. Turn left here to walk the remaining 2km back to the start, an attractive walk through scattered trees, farmland and moorland.

ROUTE 2: THE DUBLIN HILLS

Lots of moorland, forest and forest tracks on gently shelving mountains. The crossing of the narrow glacial valley of Glencullen, which consists of a mixture of upland fields and scattered housing, provides much-needed diversity. About as good a route you can get near Dublin.

Getting There: Drive through *Rockbrook*, turning left at the tee about a mile south of the village. Park almost immediately in the carpark on the left (signed Pine Forest) (GR 139227). Two variations using buses are given below. Buses to the start are 47, 47A, 47B.

Walking Time: 5.5 hours (distance 17km, climb 660m).

Difficulties: Much wet, featureless bogland, though there are a few reassurance points to help with navigation.

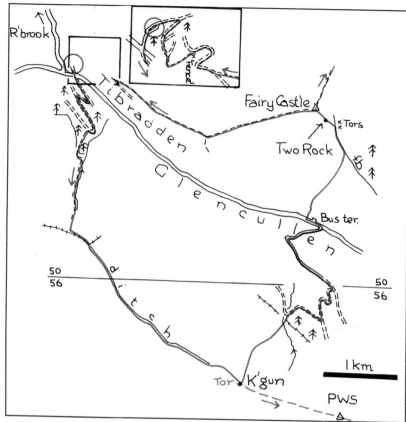

Maps: Both sheets 50 and 56. The transition is not difficult.

Route: Walk out of the carpark, cross the road and on the other side take a forest track, which climbs steeply to reveal mountain and city through scattered trees. At the tee turn left, still on an upward arc, to walk a hairpin bend to the right. A few hundred metres further on take a clear but muddy path on the left heading directly upward.

This path traverses a short stretch of thick forest to emerge at a straggly band of forest on the left. Turn left here to round this band and so reach a rough path bounding a nearby stream, onto which you turn right. The wet moorland from here on varies little for miles; on the other hand, although the scenery is hereabouts bound by the nearby horizon, it soon improves greatly to encompass most of the mountains of the north of the range. The path along the stream's bank eventually runs out. When it does, continue south for another few hundred metres to turn left at a fence roughly following the county boundary.

This fence is useful because it leads to a ditch which heads all the way to the rise to Knocknagun over 2km away to the south-east. With simple navigation you can relax and enjoy the scenery of which Lower Lough Bray tucked into its corrie and wooded Glencree, both roughly to the south, are the most notable.

The ditch is intermittent on the rise to Knocknagun, but a muddy path replaces it, so navigation continues to be simple. The path does not lead to the nondescript summit (555m, 2.5 hours); instead it ends at a gigantic tor consisting of horizontal layers of granitic rocks (1) just to its south. If you are on the bus variation ending at Enniskerry you should continue east (see below). Otherwise, a compass bearing to take you along the northern spur of Knocknagun and then down onto a tiny upland river valley might be no harm. This valley might be a good place for a rest and food; there's nowhere better for some time.

For now we are back into forest. Follow the stream to a nearby forest track, turn right and left downhill at the nearby tee. This track ends in another track and a left turn here takes you to tarmac (rudimentary tarmac initially), past tiny upland fields on the right bordered by stone walls. Cross Boranaralty Bridge to reach the R116, which runs along the northern side of Glencullen.

Turn left onto this comparatively major road, pass the bus terminus (shamefully, irresponsible citizens use it as a dump) and about 150m beyond it turn right between two closely spaced fences. The target now is Two Rock off to the north. The climb is relieved by some good scenery, albeit most of it behind into Glencullen. Head diagonally right uphill evading the occasional clump of gorse, to eventually reach the intermittent line of forest climbing the broad south-east spur of Two Rock. As it is bound by a firebreak it offers easier going. Approaching the level ground of the summit, you will observe on the right beyond a fence the two tors from which the mountain is named and on the left a heap of rocks. Walk to this heap of rocks and then continue to nearby Fairy Castle (536m), whose trig pillar is clearly visible from here.

At Fairy Castle there are two muddy and eroded paths: take the right if you intend to get the bus from the southern suburbs of the city (see below), the left if you wish to reach the starting point. This latter path heads gently downhill to the south-west. Just before scattered trees, fork right to take a path which contours along the north-eastern side of the Tibradden spur (that's all Tibradden is). With Kelly's Glen on the right this is a pleasant stretch on path, and an easy one. The path joins a track which winds down to pass a curious section of fence which looks just the thing for tethering horses (but can't be, can it?).

At this stage, we are nearly home, though surprisingly there is still room for navigational error. Keep the 'tethering fence' on the left to descend steeply on a path. Turn right at its end to walk a few metres on track, fork left shortly onto another track and continue onward (you might like to chance a direct descent along here) to take the first turn (an acute one) left and so reach to the carpark.

Bus Variation Ending at Enniskerry: From the tor walk onward along the spur (very eroded path, so don't make it worse!) to the trig pillar on Prince William's Seat. Continue east to the nearby Wicklow Way and follow it north to the road. Turn left for Kilmalin (bus 85) or Enniskerry (bus 44).

Bus Variation Ending at the Southern Suburbs: From Fairy Castle walk to Three Rock (a pin cushion of masts), continue north with forest on the left for about 700m to a track heading directly into forest. This is Tiknock Wood. From here walk downhill to the bus (44B, 47B, 48A, 75).

Note
(1) Tors: The term originates in the south-west of England where there are many such rock formations. Tors are defined as 'regions of un-kaolinised granite and are residuals left by differential denudation of the harder and softer materials'. So now you know.

ROUTE 3: THE LOUGH BRAYS AND KIPPURE

It is possible to wring a good walk out of the uncompromisingly wet and gently shelving moorland to the north of Kippure. The walk takes in the deep cleft of Mareen's Brook and the fine cliffs overlooking the large corrie lakes of the Lough Brays, thus proving that you can sometimes make a fairly decent silk purse out of a sow's ear.

Getting There: Turn left into *Glenasmole*, keeping on the main road for about 2 miles to cross a prominent concrete bridge over a water channel debouching into the nearby reservoir. Set your milometer here. At 0.4 miles pass a minor road on the left. At about 0.7 miles look out suitable places to park along the road, taking care not to block entrances. The starting point indicated on the sketch map is at the hairpin bend at the head of the road where there is space for a few carefully parked cars (GR 109199).

Walking Time: 4.75 hours (distance 14km, climb 600m).

Difficulties: Some wet ground underfoot and bracken which may be unpleasant in high summer. Navigation needs some attention but overall is not too demanding.

Map: Sheet 56, with a tiny

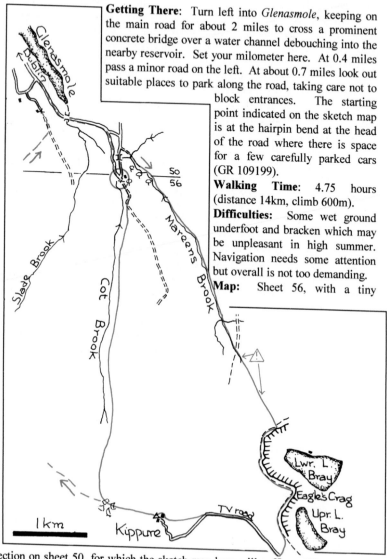

section on sheet 50, for which the sketch map here will suffice. If however you want to do the long variation, fear that you are going to go astray to the north of the route or want reassurance on the car journey take sheet 50.

Route: Let's say we are starting at the hairpin bend. Walk the untravelled leg of the bend to cross over a nearby bridge. Just beyond turn right onto a track, ignoring immediately a minor branch on the left. The track soon narrows to a

18

path and passes a footbridge on the right (don't cross it) over a river, the Dodder. Keep the Dodder on the right to cross a narrow stream (you have now walked only a few hundred metres) with the path already intermittent. From here on however, navigation is simple: all you have to do is follow the Dodder (soon to be transmogrified into Mareens Brook) on the right in a straight line south-east.

This is a surprisingly pleasant stretch: the deep-set stream plunging as an occasional low waterfall, some mature broadleaf trees on the steep opposite bank and best of all the vast acres of bogland all around - which you cannot see! Continue uphill and south-east along the Brook for about 3km, during which it gradually attains the general level of the bogland. Then, where it unravels close to its source, there intrudes an unwelcome sign of 'civilisation': the end of a bog road edged by rubbish, litter and dumping. A fine indication of our 'care' for the environment. Here, press on south-east across featureless bog to reach the edge of the cliffs overlooking Lower Lough Bray only a few hundred metres away.

The first sight of Lough Bray, its broad and usually tranquil waters, the solitary house set among trees on its shore and above all (both senses) the steep cliffs curving round to Eagle's Crag is quite dramatic.

The idea now is to turn right to follow the wide path at the edge of the cliffs to and beyond Eagle's Crag, passing on the way a deep cleft where a stream has eaten into the cliff edge. Eagle's Crag overlooks both the Lough Brays so it is worthwhile making the slight detour to take in the view. I find the Upper Lake a bit disappointing after the Lower. Maybe it lacks its variety and dramatic setting.

From Eagle's Crag keep on the path high above the Upper Lake for about another 10 minutes and then head south-west across moorland to reach the nearby TV road. From here it is an easy slog up to the summit of Kippure (757m, 3.25 hours). You need not take the road all the way - near the TV mast you can climb directly to the summit. Of Kippure, least said, soonest mended, though in its favour it might be noted that the views are extensive.

The rest of the walk is easy to describe. Though not strictly necessary, you will be sure of reaching the headwaters of the Cot Brook by walking west to the nearby col facing pt 679m and at its boggy bottom heading north. Keep the main stream somewhere on the left as you descend (the exact route is immaterial), crossing minor tributaries as you do so.

As you approach the woods, fields and houses of upper Glenasmole you will have to walk east away from the Brook to reach a track offering the only access to the road where you started. As you can see from the sketch map this track extends much further south than shown on sheet 56 and offers an easy route if the vegetation near the river becomes too trying. Turn left downhill onto the track to reach the hairpin bend.

Longer Variation: From Kippure you may be tempted to walk to Seefingan and Corrig, but I trust, only if you have sheet 50. From Corrig walk north-east to pick up a track running north-west and ending at a minor road at GR 098208. Walking time is 6.25 hours (distance 19km, climb 820m).

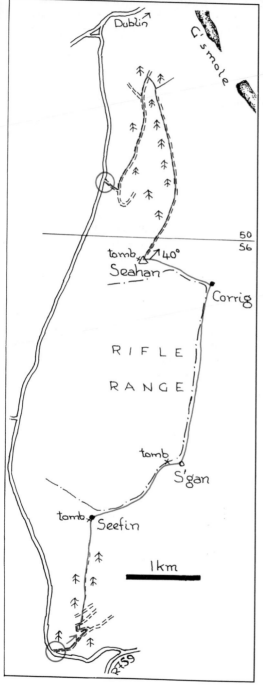

These mountains on the north-west corner of the range are gently sloped, with many areas of forestry on their lower reaches and much soft bogland higher up. However the views are expansive and the megalithic tombs on three of the summits add a touch of the exotic.

Getting There: These mountains are arranged in an uncompromisingly straight line, so this has to be an A to B route requiring two cars. Take both cars towards *Glenasmole*, but instead of turning left into it, set your milometer and continue straight. At 0.4 miles fork left. At 1.7 miles park one car at the forest entrance on the left (GR 076207). Park the second car at the forestry entrance at 5.5 miles (GR 069144), where the walk starts.

Walking Time: 4.25 hours (distance 13km, climb 620m).

Difficulties: Much soggy ground. Navigation is fairly easy.

Map: Sheets 50 and 56.

Route: Take the track from the forest entrance, keeping to the main one where a minor track branches right at a hairpin bend. Continue round one right-angle bend (to the right) and at a second, turn left uphill on a clear path and firebreak, shortly passing another track.

Now out of the trees, at least to the extent that you can see over them, views expand to include Pollaphuca Reservoir and the foothills of the mountains to the south-west. Continue upward on what is now a muddy firebreak to emerge onto the higher slopes of Seefin (621m) and walk to the modest summit, crowned by a far from modest megalithic tomb (1).

For Seefingan head east with a touch of north to drop to a shallow col and then resume the gentle but continuous climb through heather, accompanied for part of the way by old fence posts on the right. These however veer off across the slope within about 10 minutes of the summit - or rather of the huge megalithic tomb on Seefingan (724m, 1.75 hours).

In bad visibility it is important to realize that this tomb does not mark the summit of Seefingan: this is a feeble and indistinct rise in the general level of the bogland lies about 200m further east. From here, and not from the tomb, you are square with the broad ridge leading to Corrig to the north, reached on an eroded path along the county boundary and more to the point, also the boundary of the rifle range, so don't wander west. Corrig (618m), an unassuming peak, hasn't a megalithic tomb and has to make do with a modest WD marker. From here head directly to Seahan (648m, 2.75 hours), which in addition to a trig pillar has the third megalithic tomb of the day, a minor affair compared with the others. In spite of indications to the contrary on sheet 56, there are no trees on the summit of Seahan.

From Seahan head north over open ground, keeping extensive forestry on the left a little way down; a compass bearing from the summit of about 40° will allow you to meet this forestry and make the transition onto sheet 50. Once you reach it, the underfoot conditions and the navigation are easy for some time. Simply keep the forest close on the left all the way down until you enter dense trees on a rough and muddy path. This ends shortly on a track, where you turn left, and left again at the nearby junction. Walk straight ahead for about 1.5km, then turn right to reach the car, which should be visible from here.

Note
(1) Megalithic Tombs: More properly called passage graves, they date from about 2000 BC, and consist of mounds of stones with a burial chamber at the centre, entered by a long narrow passage. They are often found in groups and on summits, like those encountered on this route.

THE EAST
ROUTE 5: MAULIN AND THE TONDUFFS

A short route, through forest at first, then by Powerscourt Waterfall and the majestic bowl of the Deerpark, leading to open mountain country around memorable Maulin and the not so memorable Tonduffs. The walk ends with a steep and arduous descent alongside of the rocky buttresses of the Raven's Glen.

Getting There: Drive to *Enniskerry*, continue straight ahead (south) to pass the

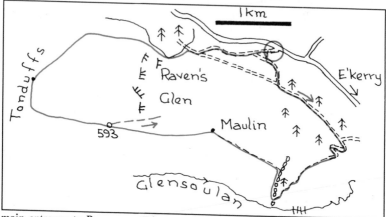

main entrance to Powerscourt, keep to the main road for 2 miles, here turning right off it at a tee. Pass the prominent gates of Powerscourt on the left and park in Crone carpark about 1 mile further on (GR 192142).

Walking Time: 4.25 hours (distance 11km, climb 580m), thus allowing about 0.5 hours extra for one steep descent.

Difficulties: Navigation generally easy. Good underfoot until the descent into the Raven's Glen, where there are steep slopes and hidden boulders which make for extremely slow progress. The variation avoids much of this difficult ground.

Map: Sheet 56.

Route: Take the track from the end of the carpark, turn immediately left onto a path, walk upwards to another track, turn left and walk to a tee, which has a Wicklow Way waymark. From here on, with only the occasional waymark to follow, you can confidently relax from detailed navigation for some time and enjoy a pleasant vista of field and forest.

Gradually forest becomes thicker and therefore the forest track more monotonous, so hopefully all burgeoning gloomy thoughts will be dispelled when you emerge from forest with the sylvan bowl of the Deerpark at your feet and a pleasant path to walk. This path leads along the edge of the Deerpark towards the mighty Powerscourt Waterfall. The path eventually enters thick forest, where it may be confused with firebreaks; keep walking roughly west if in doubt. On emerging at a tumbled stone wall, high and remote Glensoulan and the infant River Dargle are below to the left, beyond which looms the great bulk of Djouce.

However with Maulin the next goal, we are headed away from Glensoulan. Keep close to the stone wall and walk upwards until you reach the crest of the eastward spur from Maulin. Here take a prominent and unfortunately eroded path directly west to the summit.

Maulin, though a modest 570m high commands excellent views of sea, coastline and of course mountain from its position at the edge of the range. Rocky outcrops are evident on the summit of Djouce to the south and to the south-west you may be able to pick out the rim of the corrie cut into the northern side of Mullaghcleevaun.

Walk onward to a nearby shallow col just west of Maulin, clambering carefully down several rocky steps on the way. From here continue slightly uphill towards the Tonduffs, with the Raven's Glen down on the right - a somewhat intimidating sight, especially if you have decided to do the full route and so have to descend it later. For the moment however, keep to an increasingly intermittent path over featureless, soggy terrain (a compass bearing would be prudent) to attain the almost non-existent pt 593m (it's on sheet 56 if nowhere else). Point 593m (or thereabouts) has some significance, however. From here (at 2.5 hours' walking time) you can make an easy descent into the Raven's Glen by walking north-east down a long grassy tongue.

If you opt for the hard descent into the Glen, continue west on a gentle but relentless climb to the southern end of the Tonduff plateau (642m) and then swing north to the other end, walking a terrain of peat hags set in a floor of black mud. From here eastward leads over the buttresses of the Glen, so perhaps the best route is approximately north-east, though even this means slow progress over hidden boulders. As you descend aim for a stone wall beyond which are mature conifers: there is a path of sorts alongside this wall, though initially at least by no means an easy one.

The path, still by the wall, does improve as you descend, so that most resentment against the author will have dissipated (I hope) by the time you reach a forest track. Turn right onto it, and fork left shortly after to reach the start.

ROUTE 6: SALLY GAP TO MULLAGHCLEEVAUN EAST TOP

An area of bland, unimpressive mounds, much wet ground underfoot, and because of the linear layout of the high points a difficult area in which to make a convincing circuit. Still, worth walking for the excellent and expansive views towards more shapely hills to the east and south.

Getting There: By car to the carpark set back on the right off the *Military Road* about 1 mile south of Sally Gap (GR 137087). Watch out carefully for it.

Walking Time: 4.75 hours (distance 15km, climb 640m).

Difficulties: It is easy to get confused in this area of subdued moorland. However there are no cliffs and few forests. If all else fails you can always reach safety by walking east to the Military Road.

Map: Sheet 56.

Route: From the carpark head directly to Carrigvoher (682m) over shelving moorland. The rounded summit is marked by an area of stones and a ditch. The ditch runs north-east towards Sally Gap and more to the point, south-west along the route as far as the col between Gravale and Duff Hill. However it is intermittent, as is the path all along this stretch, and neither should be used as a substitute for the compass.

From Carrigvoher climb directly to Gravale, whose summit is similar to Carrigvoher's and from there to Duff Hill, which is similar to both the preceding peaks, differing only in that it has a modest boulder field on its summit. (Individuality, you will have gathered, is not a noted feature of these parts.)

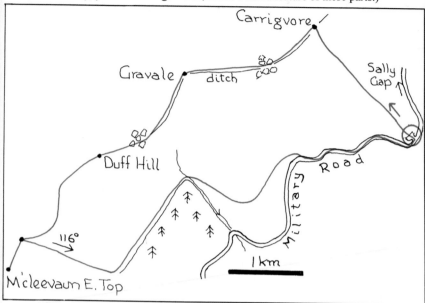

Mullaghcleevaun East Top (795m), the next target, requires a little care because it has a north top (GR 0807), with which it should not be confused. From this top it is worth pushing on to East Top proper, only 500m off to the south, as it is a good place from which to admire Mullaghcleevaun and especially the cliffs of its northern corrie.

From East Top it just about makes sense to return to the north top and from there walk along the top of a broad spur south-east (exactly 116° compass) to forest, where an ever-expanding view of Lough Dan and the peaks around it are an attractive feature. Once forest is reached head north-east along its edge, an undulating progress on a broad firebreak.

The last part of the route presents Hobson's Choice: the road or the hillside roughly parallel to it. If there is lots of traffic on the road you may elect to stay on the hill, if darkness is imminent head for the road. The carpark is not so easy to see from the hillside, so take care not to overshoot it.

Mullaghcleevaun Variation: If you have time (about 1 extra hour), it is worthwhile taking in Mullaghcleevaun. The route from East Top is easy, though it may be better to veer right of the direct route to avoid an expanse of black bog.

Two-car Variation: If you have two cars this is a much more satisfactory route. Leave the second car at the forest entrance at GR 106055, 3½ miles south along the Military Road from the carpark.

Start at the same point as the main route and follow it to East Top. From there walk south-east along a broad spur towards Carrigshouk (GR 0905, 571m), veering left off its summit to avoid crags beyond it. On the road turn left for the nearby forest entrance. Total walking time taking in the East Top but not Mullaghcleevaun is 3.75 hours (distance 11km, climb 600m).

ROUTE 7: FANCY AND KNOCKNACLOGHOGE

One of the best routes in the Wicklow mountains: a lovely interplay of rugged mountain, wooded valleys and placid (well, usually placid) lakes.

Getting There: By car drive towards *Glendalough*, turning right off the R755 onto the R759 about 7 miles south of Kilmacanoge. Drive a further 2 miles to park near the prominent set of gate pillars on the left ('Pier Gates') (GR 173064). If you are travelling by St Kevin's bus take it to the junction of the R755 and the R759 (GR 2005) and walk from there (3km extra each way).

Walking Time: 4.5 hours (distance 13km, climb 780m).

Difficulties: One usually deep stream to be forded. Otherwise easy.

Map: Sheet 56.

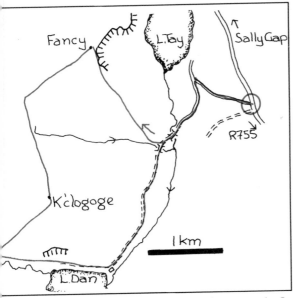

Route: From Pier Gates, you can see practically the entire route: the cliffs of Luggala topped by Fancy, bumpy Knocknacloghoge to its left, at whose foot and just out of sight lies Lough Dan. An inviting prospect!

Walk the tarmacadam road at the Gates, taking a shortcut path on the left if you wish, rather than keeping to tarmac all the way. On the valley floor and now on a track, cross one bridge and immediately turn right to follow another track westward. Leave it shortly to climb directly to the summit of Fancy (595m), a tough climb but one with widening views, best towards the summit where cliffs close on the right plunge directly in rocky precipices into Lough Tay.

Fancy's summit is a letdown: a mundane, grassy plateau. Never mind, the long views are no disappointment. From Fancy head south-west over heather towards Knocknacloghoge. Do not go directly south as this would give a difficult river crossing: it's difficult enough as it is. Once across the Brook head to the summit of Knocknacloghoge (534m), a fine, rocky point giving excellent views of Lough Dan and much more besides. To its south follow a forestry fence to reach Inchavore River at the Copse, the group of deciduous trees on the opposite bank.

Walk east from here following the river downstream to pass through a wet area below cliffs flanking the southern side of Knocknacloghoge. Here a delightful path materialises along the shore of Lough Dan. Walk it to a two-storey house close to Cloghoge River, where it improves to a track, then continue along the valley floor, all the way in splendid country, to finally face the steep uphill to Pier Gates. There had to be retribution for the initial easy downhill!

ROUTE 8: SCARR AND LOUGH DAN

Scarr is one of the most shapely peaks in Wicklow, a high hummocky grassy ridge surrounded by some of the loveliest mountain and lake country in the mountains. A short walk can easily be varied.

Getting There: Drive to *Roundwood,* turn right here to follow the signs for Lough Dan. Turn right at Oldbridge after 2½ miles, still following the signs for Lough Dan, to park a short distance beyond on waste ground on the left (GR 158018). A bus variation is given below.

Walking Time: 4.75 hours (distance 13km, climb 650m).

Difficulties: One normally fordable river to cross and another that is fordable only with difficulty. Some rough vegetation. Navigation, with the exception of two stretches detailed below, is fairly easy.

Map: Sheet 56.

Route: Walk onward from the start, taking the nearby first track on the left. This leads upward with moderately widening views. At a fork near a forestry plantation, take the right (the left is obviously about to end at a house). Walk with the forest on the left for a short distance but where the track leaves the forest edge, turn left to walk along two sides of the plantation. At the end of the second side turn left at a wide and clear firebreak to traverse a short stretch of forest and to emerge high on the spur running south-west to the summit of Scarr.

All quite mundane so far. But now a whole panorama focused on delightful Lough Dan comes into view and continues to expand as you walk up the spur on a clear path towards the summit. When you cross an earthbank you may be cheered to realize that the toil of the ascent is nearly over.

Scarr (641m) boasts marvellous views. Around the 360 degree panorama the great bulk of Tonelagee directly to the west is dominant with Glenmacnass gouged deeply out of the mountainside before it. Scarr's summit consists of a set of grassy mounds running north-south. The highest mound is always the next one along! When you have assimilated this mystery, descend steeply north-west to pick up a path which crosses the earthbank encountered earlier. Keep to the high ground past a standing stone, which might be some help in navigation, and continue beyond it in a gentle arc to the right to climb Kanturk Mountain (523m), a fascinating area of rocky hummocks with no commanding summit.

As you walk north-east along the high ground watch out for a large erratic rock, perched like a giant egg on the crest of the ridge. The aim from here is to cross Inchavore River at the Copse (GR 133046), a group of deciduous trees on the near bank; since there is forestry with severely limited access between the erratic and the Copse (the generous firebreak shown on sheet 56 does not exist), some attention to navigation is required. From the erratic walk initially roughly north-west to avoid the worst of the high heather hereabouts. At forest turn right to reach the end of the firebreak (or rough track) along its boundary. Here take the narrow path downward through the trees to the Copse (3 hours).

If you cannot cross the river here, you certainly won't be able to ford Cloghoge River later. So, if you must (or want to) shorten the walk, amble downstream to a track, fork left off it at a wooden gate onto a path, turn left at the road, and walk directly to the start. It's a lovely walk of about 1 hour.

The next section of the route is through lowland valley, with stream, lake and wooded hill close in many places: one of the loveliest stretches in Wicklow. Cross the river on fortuitously placed boulders at the Copse and head downstream along a developing path to reach the two-storey house about 2km away.

From here on, in an area of secluded paths you will have to pay some attention to navigation. Just upstream of the house cross Cloghoge River on stepping stones tantalizingly placed to make it extremely difficult to cross (1). If you can make it well and good. If not, see the variation below. On the eastern bank walk uphill between unfriendly fences to meet a path, follow it uphill to a track, turn left onto it - there's no alternative - walk a few metres, then turn right uphill just before the first dwelling onto a grassy track. Ignoring a minor track on the right at the first vee, continue uphill on the main track into an area of rough fields overlooking Lough Dan and its surrounding valleys: a lovely prospect.

Walk past a group of ruins and, just beyond them at a gate, turn right uphill to reach the corner of a forest. Turn right here onto a path hugging the forest edge and follow it into dense trees. Say goodbye to long views for a while!

A few minutes later you will reach another group of ruins set deep in the forest. Keep to the path (there's little alternative) to walk part way round the ruins and, ignoring minor paths to right and left just after them, continue onward south with a touch of east, to reach a wide forest track that offers only the occasional vista of Lough Dan down on the right. Consolation: maybe the trees will have been felled by the time you visit.

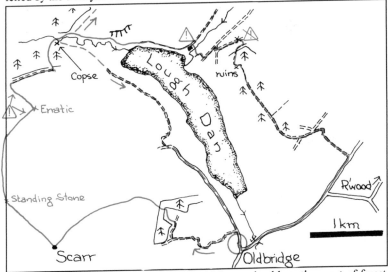

This track joins the Wicklow Way, on which you should continue out of forest and onto a good track. Turn right with the Way onto tarmac and walk mostly downhill all the way back to the start.

Bus Variation: Alight from the St Kevin's Bus at the first junction right south of Roundwood, take minor roads to the start of the walk proper at Oldbridge (GR 1501). Follow the above route to the summit of Scarr (2.5 hours), here take route 16 into Laragh, from where you can catch the evening bus. Walking time is 4 hours (distance 13km, climb 500m).

Longer Variation: This is a lovely extension to the walk. From the Copse climb Knocknacloghoge, walk north to reach a grassy track, descend east to the track running along the valley of Cloghoge River, ford the river at the two-storey house. Additional walking time is 2 hours (distance 5km, climb 340m).

Variation at Cloghoge River: If you cannot cross the river, take the track to Pier Gates (GR 173064), and then the Wicklow Way to the start. This is not as scenic as the main route. Walking time from the stepping stones is 3 hours (distance 11km, climb 300m).

Note

(1) Don't forget you can wade across. To do this, take off your boots and socks, put your boots on again, wade, pour the water out of your boots (important!), dry your feet, put your socks and boots on again. Unpleasant but simple.

ROUTE 9: DJOUCE AND WAR HILL

After a slightly dull start, a varied and easy walk with lovely, wide views from the southern spur of Djouce. It is followed by a stroll along the banks of Dargle River in the heart of narrow Glensoulan. Perhaps a bit short for summer but ideal for short winter days.

Getting There: Drive to *Enniskerry*, pass the main entrance to Powerscourt, turn right off the main road (signed 'Roundwood') after 2 miles, drive for a further 2.5 miles to park in the third of Djouce Woods carparks (GR 210107). This carpark is a little further south than shown on sheet 56.

Walking Time: 4.25 hours (distance 13km, climb 550m).

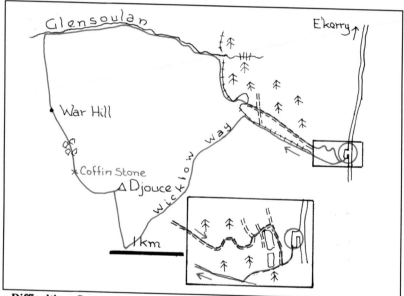

Difficulties: Some wet and eroded ground; easy navigationally.

Map: Sheet 56.

Route: Take the path from the carpark, cross a stream and climb westward into forest, crossing a fence on the left after a few hundred metres from the stream to reach open country east of Djouce. Keeping forest on the right ascend slowly north-westwards to the crest of the hill, where you will meet a Wicklow Way waymark. Turn left here onto the Way.

It hasn't been very exciting so far. But now on the eastern shoulder of Djouce and with views opening up particularly over the plateau of Calary, prospects start to improve. Keep on the Wicklow Way, forking left with it where a horrible path has been gouged directly to the summit (please don't take it). The Way continues first on the level and then uphill to reach the crest of the long spur running south from Djouce.

From here to Djouce is a glorious stretch, with a wide panorama of peaks crowding the south and west horizons. The whole of this section is marked by a path, so the only point to pay attention to is to swing right on the summit plateau. Djouce's summit (725m) is marked by a trig pillar and several fangs of mica-schist rock rearing skyward. The views, encompassing a wide range of mountain and the coastal plain north and south of Dublin are excellent.

From Djouce head initially west for a few hundred metres and then swing right to follow the high ground and a set of rusty iron posts north-west to the Coffin Stone. This enormous boulder certainly has an appropriate name; it is coffin-shaped, though much bigger than life-size (so to speak). A good sheltered place for food.

Continue north to the eroded, muddy col facing War Hill, and walk from there to the summit, a modest few stones on an area of undistinguished bog. From here you can aim anywhere from north to north-east, the simple object being to reach Dargle River in Glensoulan. On the way down you should be able to spot the remains of Grouse House (1) away to the west, a stark chimney in a stark landscape. Turn right downstream when you reach the river, and follow the bank along the narrow steep-sided valley, its austerity softened by the occasional ancient tree clinging to its slopes. A delightful stretch.

When you reach a forestry plantation, turn steeply uphill to follow the forest edge on the left. Look out for a significant unplanted indentation in the forest about 500m (distance, not height!) from the river. Turn left here to walk diagonally across the indentation, where you should pick up a path that heads roughly east into forest and shortly improves to a track.

Follow this track straight ahead through forest and after a few zig-zags, take a path on the right running steeply downhill to reach a section of the same track running at right angles to the section you are on (if you reckon that life is too short to work out this complicated description, the sketch map might help). Follow this section of track across the low ground left by the deceased Paddock Pond (2). Turn right at the far side of the low ground to walk along its length. At its southern end, with private property ahead turn left uphill to reach the carpark.

Notes
(1) Grouse House, of which only the chimney remains, was once a hunting lodge.
(2) Paddock Pond was a reservoir. In 1986 there was a cloudburst in this area during which waters of the Pond broke through their impounding wall, leaving this low, reedy area.

ROUTE 10: DJOUCE AND FANCY

Excellent views over much of the route, with especially good, varied angles on Lough Tay snuggled below the great cliffs of Luggala. The centre section has some difficult vegetation underfoot and rather too much moorland.

Getting There: Turn right at *Kilmacanoge* onto the R755, turn right again after 7 miles onto the R759. Continue uphill for 2.7 miles, parking in the second of two closely spaced carparks on the right (GR 169074). This point may also be easily reached from Sally Gap.

Walking Time: 5.25 hours (distance 16km, climb 760m).

Difficulties: As well as being rough underfoot as already mentioned, the centre section around the R759 is also the section which requires some attention to navigation.

Map: Sheet 56.

Route: From the carpark turn left to walk south along the road, a walk enlivened by the sight of Lough Tay tucked in below the cliffs of Fancy down on the right. There are plenty of other lovely views of Lough Tay before the end of the walk.

After 1km turn right at a set of high pillars ('Pier Gates') to face the cliffs terminating the eastern side of Fancy. Walk the road beyond the pillars to reach the floor of the valley (you may like to take a short cut on a rough path to shorten the journey). On the valley floor and now in the midst of some of the most delectable scenery in Wicklow (or anywhere else for that matter), cross one bridge, turn right onto a side track just beyond it and veer right from the narrow, wooded valley ahead to start the steep climb to Fancy to the north-west.

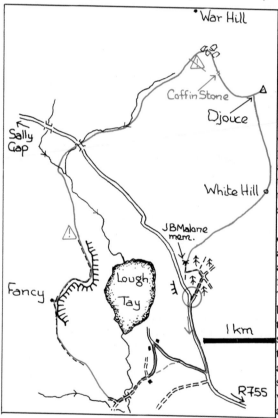

As you ascend you should pick up a path, clearer on the higher slopes, which will take you along the mighty cliffs overlooking Lough Tay and to the summit itself, a modest 595m high with surprisingly, an equally modest summit plateau of rough heather and grass, this in spite of the dramatic nature of the cliffs so close to the summit.

From the summit continue on the path along the cliff edge, thus avoiding high vegetation for as long as possible. The path gradually becomes intermittent on the descent from Fancy, so it might be some help to say that it runs roughly above the scattered trees spreading up from the valley floor. As you approach the road you will see the next target, the prominent bridge at GR 148 096, reached by walking the bank of Cloghoge River and then fording one of its branches. Around here there are, incidentally, excellent sheltered places to stop for a break.

At 2.75 hours into the walk and with the car only 3km by road (hope you aren't tempted), cross the road and continue up the narrow and pleasant river valley beyond for a few hundred metres, then veer east to cross wet moorland and so reach the col between Djouce and War Hill.

30

At the col turn south to follow a set of iron fence posts (no wire) past the Coffin Stone, a useful reassurance point as the stone fully lives up to its name. Beyond it climb to the western side of Djouce's summit plateau, swinging left on it to reach the fangs of rock and the trig pillar which crowns it.

From Djouce the rest is easy, both physically and navigationally and in addition offers lovely views, especially to the west towards the high peaks of Mullaghcleevaun and Tonelagee. Retrace your steps south-west from the summit for 100m or so and then swing south down the southern shoulder of Djouce. After less than 1km you will pick up the Wicklow Way and since it is to be followed to the end, navigational problems are behind - unless of course the route of the Way is altered.

With this possibility in mind a few directions are prudent. Follow the Way over hummocky terrain at White Hill and down past the JB Malone memorial, around where there are renewed splendid vistas of Lough Tay. Turn left at forest and briefly enter it. Turn right at a nearby cross tracks to reach the nearby carpark.

ROUTE 11: BARNACULLIAN RIDGE AND TONELAGEE

Lovely, spectacular scenery on the descent from Tonelagee and good, but not quite so spectacular scenery on the ascent onto the broad Barnacullian ridge. The ridge forms the central part of the walk and gives excellent long views, but the soft terrain here makes for slow going.

Getting There: By car to *Sally Gap*, and thence onward along the Military Road to the large Glenmacnass carpark (GR 114029), about 7 miles to the south. The total distance from central Dublin is about 24 miles.

Walking Time: 4 hours (distance 12km, climb 520m).

Difficulties: Much wet ground on the Barnacullian ridge. On the ridge the reassuring Military Road is always somewhere to the east, but so are some stretches of cliff. Navigationally therefore, the route requires a little care. At the end of the walk Glenmacnass River may be difficult to ford, especially after rain. At the start have a look at the usual crossing point about 70m upstream of the carpark and see if you are going to be able to cross it at the end.

Map: Sheet 56.

Route: From the carpark walk upstream .... for miles and miles. A riverside walk with the forestry plantations not as oppressive as they appear on the OS map, this stretch makes for easy walking and a steady increase in wildness and remoteness. At length (5km to be approximate), you will arrive at the bottom of steep, rock-strewn ground over which the infant Glenmacnass River cascades. There is nothing for it now but to climb alongside the stream to the Barnacullian ridge to the west (yes, your premonition was correct).

On the sloping eastern side of the ridge, which doesn't seem much like a ridge at this stage, head roughly south to cross a nearby stile in a fence. From here on, keep to this side of the crest of the ridge on a narrow band of grass bordering the large expanse of mud covering the top. Alternatively, there is nothing to prevent your walking boldly down the centre of the ridge, bar the fear of being sucked into the bog of course. If you do so walk, note that the only indication of the peak marked on the map as Barnacullian is a signpost, but alas no sign.

South of Barnacullian the ridge narrows slightly and simultaneously dips into a particularly wet area, one where peat hags will cause unwanted detours. Beyond this dip climb directly to Stoney Top (714m), the northern satellite of Tonelagee.

From here the climb to Tonelagee is steep, but navigationally easy on a clear path; the views over Lough Ouler are magnificent. Near the summit note the standing stone overlooking the lough, because from here you can make a steep descent to the lake on the return (see below). Tonelagee (3.25 hours) is one of the finest summits in Wicklow: the third highest at 817m, commanding magnificent views in all directions and with the great corrie containing Lough Ouler gouged out of its north-eastern flank.

From Tonelagee, if you have decided against the direct descent to Lough Ouler described below, take the north-eastern spur to descend steeply, the heart-shaped lough down on the left. Then climb about 30m to pt 668m. From here a compass bearing of 66° will take you directly down to the carpark across easy, fairly dry ground (for some mysterious reason my intuition tends to direct me to the right of the correct bearing). When you reach Glenmacnass River look out for a set of naturally-placed stones about 70m upstream of the carpark and cross there.

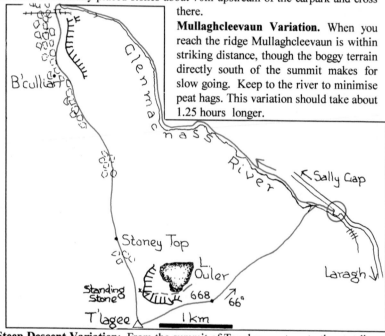

Mullaghcleevaun Variation. When you reach the ridge Mullaghcleevaun is within striking distance, though the boggy terrain directly south of the summit makes for slow going. Keep to the river to minimise peat hags. This variation should take about 1.25 hours longer.

Steep Descent Variation: From the summit of Tonelagee return to the standing stone. From it walk the few metres directly to the cliffs and then look right where there is a grassy gully at your feet. This is the descent route to the lake, and it is here at the top at its steepest.

THE SOUTH-EAST

ROUTE 12: CROGHAN MOUNTAIN

An easy but not over-exciting walk along the length of an isolated outlier well to the south of the main range. Quite a wealth of varied scenery on offer: rich farmland and a long stretch of coast as well as the bulk of the mountains to the north, culminating in not so far off Lugnaquillia.

Getting There: Let's say you are starting north of the main bridge in Aughrim (GR 1279). Cross the bridge, turn right onto the R747. Turn left (signposted 'Toberpatrick') after over 3 miles and left again at the tee. Turn sharply first right, pass two tracks on the left and park on waste ground a few hundred metres beyond the second (GR 105737), where there is space for a few cars.

Walking Time: 3.5 hours (distance 10km, climb 540m).

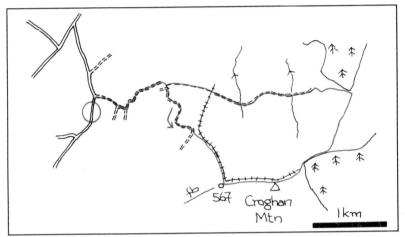

Difficulties: None.

Map: Sheet 62.

Route: Walk back to the first track (to dispel ambiguity: I mean the first met after alighting from the car), take it to a tee and turn left uphill. The track is quite muddy so you might greet its end in a field at the crest of the hill with some relief. Here the north-west spur of Croghan Mountain, the first goal, is off to the right and the navigation obvious.

Cross the field and climb, but before you do so, note this field as it is important for the return. There is an ugly new forestry track which is easier to walk than high heather, but sooner or later you will want to leave it and climb directly to the West Top (567m) from where the main summit (606m), crowned by a dwarf trig pillar and several rocky outcrops, is but a short walk away.

Having assimilated the view, and it covers a wide expanse of country, walk north-east to meet a block of forest and keeping it on the right follow a track along its edge. Where the edge swings decisively right walk north downhill to meet the near corner of another block of forest, this one partly clear-felled and with some of its trees blown over.

And here it is time, maybe you think prematurely, to head for home. You can walk onward to pt 427m to the north, but the ground is rough and the rewards scanty, so it is hardly worth doing.

Keeping the block of forest on the right head downhill, veering away from its edge to follow a wall bounding upland fields. Round one corner of the wall and then pick up a grassy track, which shortly crosses a stream issuing from a half-hearted corrie lightly etched into the northern side of Croghan. Follow the track to a fence and beyond it continue on a path, upland fields still on the right, to the crest of the hill; yes, the same hill that you started up earlier in the day with the same field to cross to meet the same track that you started up on.   Don't be tempted, by the way, to continue directly downhill on the forestry track reached before you cross the field: it doesn't lead home.

So all that remains now is to follow the track back, not forgetting to turn right to reach tarmac and of course to turn left onto it.

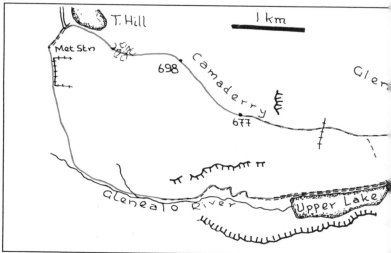

ROUTE 13:   CAMADERRY

A short route in one of the most attractive areas in Wicklow. Camaderry is the imposing summit which rises directly ahead on the road from Laragh to Glendalough, like the prow of an upturned boat. The route traverses part of the two valleys, Glendasan and Glendalough, which lie to its right and left respectively and (of course) tackles Camaderry itself.

Getting There: Drive to *Glendalough,* pass the Royal Hotel and park in the carpark on the right just after it (GR 123969). This is a popular parking spot so it may be necessary to park somewhere else around.

Walking Time: 5.25 hours (distance 16km, climb 640m).

Difficulties: None.

Map: Sheet 56 or the National Park's 1:25 000 map.

Route: From the carpark walk west (away from the road bridge) and shortly turn first right onto a track. In a minute or so you will be in Glendasan, its river on the right and rising fields on the left: a peaceful haven, and a world away from busy Glendalough.

After crossing a forest bar, look for stepping stones across the river. Walk onward along the track for another minute or so and here take a path on the left heading directly up through trees. If you miss it it doesn't really matter as the idea is to reach a grassy track running gently diagonally uphill and you can easily walk between the trees, path or no path. When you reach the track turn left onto it and follow it out of forest and into an area with fields on the left, the same fields you passed earlier. At these fields the track narrows to a path, and shortly ends at a forest track, onto which you turn right.

(An aside. From here to the south-east summit of Camaderry over two kilometres away the scenery is excellent: Glendalough down on the left, the great bulk of Tonelagee to the right and a gradually expanding circuit of mountains revealing themselves in all directions: all of which should divert you from the pain of the steady climb.)

But back to the route description. Follow the track upwards to nearly its end at a turning circle. Just before the circle take a path on the right heading westward and upward towards the south-east summit. At length you will cross a fence and face a steeper climb to this summit, still on the path. As it is fairly eroded here, try not to make it worse.

The south-east summit (677m) is not over impressive though the views are excellent. From here walk to the north-west summit (698m), from where the views west are not improved by the ramparts of Turlough Hill (1), though they are splendid in other directions. Drop to an area of peat hags west of the north-west summit and from there continue to Turlough Hill, keeping it on the right.

After walking part way round its ramparts you will come to a tarmac road, with a rough track heading off south-west from it. Take this track to reach a small building, the remains of a met station. Head south from here, initially following a fence on the left, down a broad tongue of heathery country reaching towards the upper Glenealo valley. When you reach the eastward-running main stream in the valley, Glenealo River itself, turn left. (It's difficult to mistake this river as the land rises steeply from its other bank.)

Once at the river the rest is easy: simply follow it down and east keeping to the near bank. This is a pleasant stretch along a seemingly remote valley, though in fact it is only a few kilometres from Glendalough itself. As you progress the cliffs of Camaderry and the Spink to left and right respectively become increasingly imposing until eventually you are abreast of them and face a steep descent on a good zig-zag track towards the Upper Lake. This track will take you along the shores of the lake and to the large carpark at its eastern end. Walk south through the carpark to reach a track close to steep wooded ground on the edge of the valley. Turn left onto it and walk past the Lower Lake through an oakwood, an easy pleasant walk. Cross the first bridge encountered to pass through the cemetery containing the Round Tower and so reach the carpark.

Note

(1) At first glance the economics of this electricity station are extremely odd. At night the generators pump water up from the lower lake (Lough Nahanagan) and so the station consumes electricity. By day the water is allowed to flow back down to Lough Nahanagan through the turbines and so produce electricity. But the amount of electricity generated in the day is far less than the amount consumed at night! Nevertheless this does make economic sense because the station uses electricity at night when it is cheap and generates electricity during the peak period of the day when it is much dearer

ROUTE 14: CIRCUIT OF GLENDALOUGH

The upper valley of Glendalough is bordered north and south by bold peaks offering lovely views in all directions. Fairly good terrain throughout except for one area of wet ground towards the middle of the circuit. A long route though one which may be easily shortened.

Getting There: By car to the upper carpark, *Glendalough* (GR 112964). A small charge is payable into the carpark; parking is not permitted on the narrow approach road.

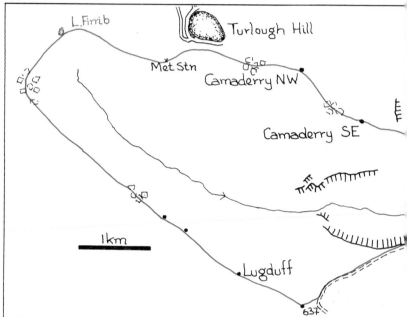

St Kevin's bus to its terminus. From there cross the road bridge in the village, walk through the cemetery containing the Round Tower, cross the footbridge to its south, turn right and walk the track to the information office just south of the upper carpark. This is a lovely, easy walk which adds about 1.5km each way.

Walking Time: 6 hours (distance 17km, climb 840m) with several opportunities to shorten.

Difficulties: One section of the route is difficult navigationally in bad weather; otherwise easy. Generally good underfoot.

Map: Sheet 56 or the National Park's 1:25 000 Glendalough map, though the latter does not show a small section of the extreme west of the route, which is of course the most difficult section to navigate. Conclusion: don't use this map in bad weather.

Route: You can see a lot of the route from the carpark; in particular your gaze will be drawn to the wooded Spink rising precipitously from the southern shores of the Upper Lake. An enticing initial goal!

From the carpark walk south to cross a bridge and climb by a path through mature trees, keeping the surging Pollanass Waterfall close on the left. Where the path ends at a forest track, continue steadily upward to where forest tracks diverge in all directions. Turn sharply right here climbing still, and now in open forest, walk to the first hairpin bend, a left, where there is a stile on the right.

The climb to the crest of the Spink is at hand. Cross the stile and take any of the rough paths beyond to the highest point on the skyline ahead. And here at the skyline is the start of the walk west along the Spink: cliffs plunging on the right to the Upper Lake, a partly wooded upland valley on the left and all around a great mass of striking mountains. Sheer delight. But remember this is an eroded path, so please try not to make it any worse.

Follow the generally rising path west high above the shores of the Upper Lake and continue beyond the lake where the path improves to a track. This track swings left and upward towards Lugduff East (637m). Towards but not to, so at

about the highest point of the track you must leave it and walk the short distance uphill to the summit, crowned by a modest cairn.

From here the route is virtually a straight line on a path all the way to the far end of the Lugduffs, and what a magnificent walk it is! The great Lugnaquillia massif to the south, Camaderry to the north - only the ramparts of Turlough Hill mar the view. It's easy walking, the landmarks being Lugduff (652m), whose cairn boasts a few white quartzite boulders, and the more indeterminate stretch of high ground called Lugduff West (607m).

At the end of all this, descend an obvious 50m and, now at a high col with about 3 hours' walking time under your belt and with the prospect of tougher and less rewarding terrain ahead, you can conveniently opt out by returning along the north bank of Glenealo River. If however you want to push on continue north-west gently uphill, still on a path as far as pt 633m. Walk onwards to Conavalla's north-east top (702m), an indistinct rise crowned by a small cairn in the middle of peat hags and not easy to find in bad visibility.

The next landmark, Lough Firrib, is equally difficult to find, and not only in bad visibility, though the present approach from higher ground offers a better chance than from most. A small lake tucked into the midst of rolling moorland, it is a good place to have a rest and a bite to eat.

Route navigation from here on is easier. There is a intermittent trench to the ramparts of Turlough Hill; keep them on your left. Beyond Turlough Hill descend to a broad col facing Camaderry, a col broken up by peat hags. This is another decision point: you can walk from here down to Glenealo River, but not from further on. There is a fairly short climb to the summit of Camaderry north-west top (698m) and scarcely any rise to Camaderry south-east top (677m). Neither of these summits is particularly impressive though the views from both are splendid. The descent from the south-east top is on an eroded path, which crosses a fence before swinging right directly downhill towards the carpark. Take care on this steep descent: it's easy to slip when tired at the end of a long day.

ROUTE 15: DERRYBAWN AND THE SPINK

A short walk, though you can easily extend it, in some of the most magnificent country in Wicklow: Derrybawn and the Spink are both narrow, rocky ridges and both offer varying panoramas over lovely mountain scenery.

Getting There: Park in the Upper Carpark *Glendalough* or walk there from the St Kevin's bus terminus in Glendalough. Further details are given under route 14.

Walking Time: 4 hours (distance 10km, climb 680m).

Difficulties: Take care on the slippery rocks of the Spink and try not to cause any more erosion here on an already eroded path. Navigation is easy.

Map: Sheet 56. The National Park's 1:25 000 sheet also covers the route more than adequately and shows paths and tracks clearer than does sheet 56.

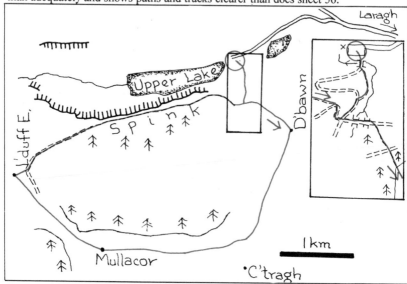

Route: From the carpark walk south to cross a sward and beyond it take a path beside the surging Pollanass Waterfall. At the top of the path continue upward on a track for a short distance, then turn first left to cross two nearby closely spaced bridges. So far, so easy.

Somewhat sterner stuff lies ahead. Just past the bridges take a path on the right heading diagonally upward through young trees. It crosses a forest track and continues straight and steeply up beyond it through mature trees to emerge from forest into open ground just west of Derrybawn. Continue upward, still on the path to the summit cairn (474m).

All the while from the start the scenery has been good and ever widening. And now from the summit onward a wide panorama of high mountains is revealed in all directions, a panorama which will be enhanced in the walk ahead.

From the summit walk south-west along the narrow, rocky Derrybawn ridge, the finest in Wicklow, though admittedly Wicklow is not particularly noted for its ridges. At its end after about 1.5km cross the end of a rough track to face moorland. The general idea now is reach the left-most corner of mature trees near at hand to the west, to which there is a rough path.

At this corner follow the fence away from forest to reach a convenient place to cross and then head towards the summit of Mullacor, a path and soft grass making for easy going. This section is gently upward all the way except for one level area, which you should not confuse for the summit in bad visibility. The summit (657m, 2.5 hours) is also flat, but has an unmistakable drop after it.

From Mullacor continue downhill north-west to a grassy col with forestry close at hand to north and south and then climb to Lugduff East (637m). This is the point at which you can decide to extend the walk (see below). If you don't want to, head north-east from the summit to turn left onto a wide firebreak (or maybe it is a track) bordering an expanse of forest in various stages of growth (its ragged edge is shown as a neat line on sheet 56).

From here on navigation is simple and you can concentrate on some of the finest views in the entire mountain area. Simply keep to the track, which gradually narrows to a path and heads east along the Spink. Along here the cliffs overlooking Glendalough are at your feet with others facing you across the deep, narrow valley to its north, while on the right a fringe of trees fronts a partly-wooded upland valley.

The walk along the Spink is about 2km long, and is lovely all the way. When the ground begins to drop steeply ahead, keep an eye out for a path heading down through scattered trees on the right (if you completely miss this path do not despair: you can continue directly down though it is pretty steep). On the path walk diagonally downhill to a solid stile beyond which is a forest track. Turn left onto it to reach a spaghetti junction of forest tracks, which you should recognise from earlier in the day. Turn left and walk downhill to the carpark.

Longer Variation: From Lugduff East you can continue along the Lugduff ridge to the col facing Conavalla, as described under route 14. From there you can descend to Glenealo River, cross it and walk all the way downhill into Glendalough. The walking time from Lugduff East is 2 hours.

ROUTE 16: TONELAGEE AND SCARR

Two of the most majestic mountains in Wicklow are climbed from the undulating and in places rocky mounds of the Brockaghs, with a leisurely return along the long southern flank of Scarr. Excellent long-distance views throughout. This is a long walk, though the variation is much shorter.

Getting There: Drive to *Laragh,* cross the main bridge in the village, fork right immediately (towards Glendalough) and shortly turn right just before McCoy's shop. Drive to the nearby forest entrance on the right (GR 139968).

St Kevin's bus to Laragh. Note that with the present timetable only the short variation is feasible.

Walking Time: 7.75 hours (distance 22km, climb 1120m).

Difficulties: Take care not to get lost on the complicated tracks and paths at the start and on the Brockaghs where there are few distinct landmarks. One river which may be difficult to ford after severe rain.

Map: Sheet 56, with the National Park's Glendalough map useful on the forest tracks at the start, though it does not cover the northern part of the route.

Route: Walk a few metres onward from the forest entrance, here taking a track on the right. At the three-way fork a little way up take the centre track, that is to the left of the house. It soon degenerates to a path barred by several gates and passes a derelict house on the left. Continue upwards on what is now a grassy path, bound by fields on the right, to reach a gate with a forest track beyond. Continue straight ahead on the forest track for 100m or so, where there is a break in the thick forest on the left. And that's the first kilometre or so of the route under your belt!

At the break take the path upwards, and now on the southern slopes of the southern Brockagh (470m) with open ground from here on, you can afford to relax a little. But only a little, since the Brockaghs demand fairly careful navigation. In bad weather each of the four mounds on the generally north-west running, undulating spur demands its own bearing, and with lovely views in all directions it is difficult to bother about navigation. The southern Brockagh is crowned by a group of huge rounded boulders, the second (557m) by a cairn (useful in an area where there are few), while the third and fourth (pts 548m and 546m) are even less distinct than the previous tops. However the wet basin containing a small lake 500m to the east of the fourth Brockagh is a useful landmark.

Even if you miss this Brockagh you won't miss the steep and lengthy rise to Tonelagee. Climb to the trig pillar on the summit (817m, 3.75 hours), from where the views are predictably magnificent: the great Lugnaquillia massif to the south, the knobbly peaks of Fancy and Knocknacloghoge to the east with lofty Scarr to its right.

Scarr, on the far side of the Military road, is the next target. Descend Tonelagee's eastern spur, the great corrie on the left plunging in grassy cliffs to heart-shaped Lough Ouler and climb 30m or so to reach pt 668m, an important summit if you are on the short variation (see below). Continue north-east on an increasingly indeterminate spur, aiming for the large carpark at Glenmacnass (GR 114030). Well, not quite the carpark: cross the river on rough stepping stones about 70m upstream and walk to the carpark.

Cross the road here and head uphill eastward towards the first of the rocky hummocks of Kanturk Mountain. Once they are in sight swing right following a

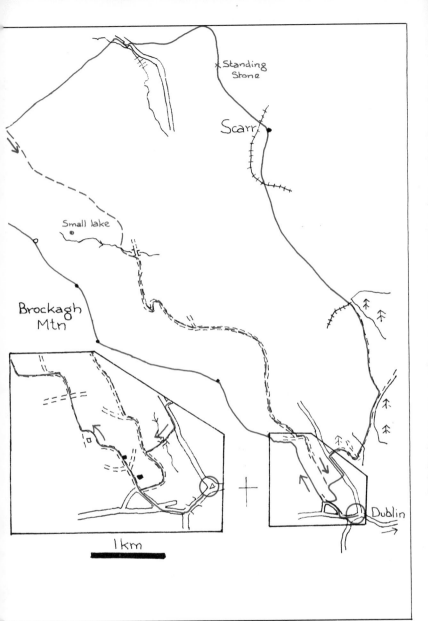

1 km

path to face the long north-western spur of Scarr. Pass a standing stone (it may be a useful landmark) and continue along the high ground to the fence and earthbank close to the summit. From here the summit itself (6.25 hours), described in route 8, is a short but steep climb.

The rest is easy: a lovely walk over high ground with a wealth of mountain scenery all round. Walk initially south from Scarr along the crest of the spur for about 2km to reach a forest corner. Cross a dilapidated fence here, just beyond which you will see ahead a track running alongside the forest and a rutted track forking off to the right. Follow the clear path between the two.

This path takes you south down the crest of the broad spur to another block of forest, where you join the Wicklow Way by turning right. The Way is to be followed to the start; this brief description relates to its present (1996) route. Descend through rough upland pastures into forest to reach a track. Turn left here to gain tarmac. Turn left again and shortly right to cross Glenmacnass River on a sturdy footbridge. Again out of forest turn left and walk the short distance to the start.

Short Variation: From pt 668m descend south-east over high ground for 2km. Just before the first stream turn left to reach a forest track visible from here. Turn right onto it and follow it all the way down to the forest entrance, turning left to keep on the main track at the one point where there may be some doubt. Total walking time is 6.25 hours (distance 18km, climb 840m).

ROUTE 17: LUGNAQUILLIA FROM GLENMALURE

This is only one of several delightful routes from Glenmalure to Lug. A steep climb partly alongside the rapids of the stern Fraughan Rock Glen ends close to the summit, with a return over easy ground giving lovely, long-distance views.

Getting There: By car to *Drumgoff crossroads*. Turn right here and drive about another 3 miles, parking in the large carpark at the head of the valley at Baravore (GR 065942).

Walking Time: 5.25 hours (distance 15km, climb 780m).

Difficulties: Some attention to navigation required on the descents from Clohernagh and from Art's Lough. Otherwise quite easy, though this is an area with several sections of cliff so mistakes could be serious.

Map: Sheet 56. It shows forest tracks incorrectly.

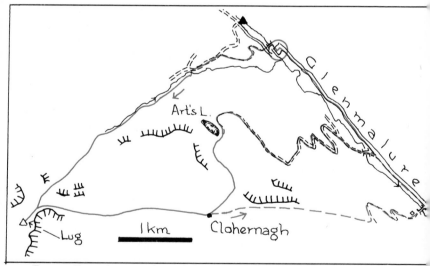

Route: From the carpark cross the river on a footbridge a little upstream and directly opposite plunge into forest on a wide path running uphill. This path shortly passes a fine stone building and ends on a forest track. Turn left here to continue uphill to a junction, one track continuing straight ahead, the other bending sharply right. Ford the river on the left (it may be difficult after rain) and, now in the open terrain of Fraughan Rock Glen, continue uphill keeping between fence and river to avoid private property.

The scenery, already majestic as you entered open country, improves as you advance. Climb by the side of the rapids terminating the Glen, the cliffs of Ben Leagh and those close to Art's Lough towering above you to right and left respectively. This climb ends in a soggy valley. Cross it, still following the main stream south-westwards, and make your way through boulders upward into an area where the ground is undulating but overall generally rising. Above it, and still to the south-west, lies the plateau crowned by the summit of Lugnaquillia.

Once on the plateau head directly gently uphill over short grass to the huge cairn marking the summit (2.75 hours). At 925m this is the sixth-highest peak in Ireland and the highest in Wicklow. In good weather the views of mountains in all directions are magnificent, those to the north being particularly fine. Maybe you can see the TV mast on Mount Leinster, about 45km away - this shouldn't be too difficult since a reliable friend claims to have seen the Reeks, fully 260km away.

From Lug one bearing will take you directly over easy terrain to Clohernagh - or rather, it would if the cliffs of the South Prison didn't intrude. So you can start off on a direct bearing, veer initially left from it to avoid plunging over the cliffs and shortly after resume that bearing. The scenery on this high-level stretch to Clohernagh is lovely, almost as good as from Lug itself.

Clohernagh (800m) presents only a minor rise, so it is just as well that it has a large cairn. The descent to Art's Lough is a bit tricky navigationally, so in bad visibility it might be prudent to head for the top of the zig-zags (see below). In good weather walk on a compass bearing of about 50° for about 500m to avoid steep ground, then swing left to walk down a grassy ramp to Art's Lough.

The lake is perched on the edge of steep ground running down to Fraughan Rock Glen and overlooked to the south-west by rocky cliffs - a striking location. Curiously, it appears to have no inlet or outlet stream. The latter runs initially underground north-westward to cascade into Fraughan Rock Glen.

The end of a forest track (not marked on sheet 56) is only a few hundred metres east of Art's Lough. You can walk directly over high heather to it but in good visibility cross a fence running north on the lake's north-east side to turn left and follow a path. It initially parallels the fence but shortly veers away from it to end at the forest track. And from here it is simply a matter of following the main track downhill, ignoring what are obviously minor tracks. On the valley floor, turn left onto the road and walk 2km back to the carpark.

Descent to the Zig-Zags Track: Walk east from Clohernagh to reach the Bendoo cliffs on the left. Keep walking east to pick up a track, indistinct in its higher reaches (if you fail initially to find it, walk directly downhill a few hundred metres west of Carrawaystick Brook, a major stream). Walk by a farmhouse, taking great care to respect the privacy of the occupiers, to reach the road. Walking time from Clohernagh to the road is 0.75 hours.

ROUTE 18: CARRAWAYSTICK AND CROAGH-ANMOIRA

The high points of this route are the sombre beauty of Kelly's Lough, the classical pyramid of Croaghanmoira and a delightful stroll along the rocky Fananieren ridge. Elsewhere views are marred by great expanses of dreary conifers lapping the lower slopes of the mountains around.

Getting There: Drive to *Drumgoff crossroads*, turn left here and park immediately in the carpark on the right (GR 106908). It should be pointed out that this is not a public carpark but belongs to the hotel and pub opposite. The owners would welcome your patronage at the end of the walk.

Walking Time: 6.75 hours (distance 20km, climb 920m).

Difficulties: With vast swathes of impenetrable forest in many areas this is not the easiest route to navigate. Underfoot generally good, with much forest track.

Maps: Sheets 56 and 62, with an awkward transition from one to the other. The depiction of forest tracks and forestry on both sheets is quite inaccurate.

Route: Follow the Wicklow Way south from the crossroads onto a forest track on

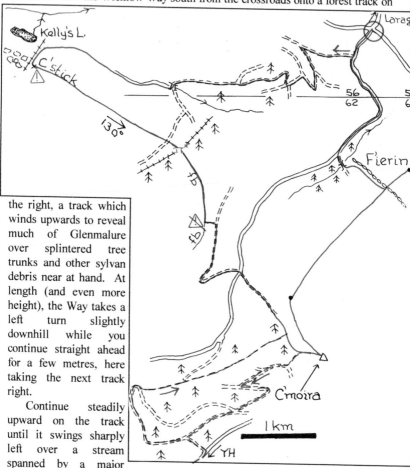

the right, a track which winds upwards to reveal much of Glenmalure over splintered tree trunks and other sylvan debris near at hand. At length (and even more height), the Way takes a left turn slightly downhill while you continue straight ahead for a few metres, here taking the next track right.

Continue steadily upward on the track until it swings sharply left over a stream spanned by a major bridge. The idea now is to walk upstream through young trees, passing a forest track on the way to the stream's source. This is tough going, so you may prefer to keep to the track and fork first right to reach this point. In either case continue moderately uphill to the shallow col beyond the source of the stream. This col, overlooking Kelly's Lough, is a nice scenic spot for a break. Kelly's Lough is one of the largest of the upland lakes and is set in a lovely location: the Lugnaquillia massif behind, Clohernagh rising majestically to the north with the

44

steep ground below Carrawaystick on the other side.

It is to the spur called Carrawaystick to which we must now turn our attention. From the col head diagonally right uphill to meet a fence running directly to the crest of the spur, which (at about GR 058905) is topped by peat hags and a small cross commemorating two men killed in a plane crash in 1992 (2.75 hours).

From the cross take a compass bearing of about 130° over 2.5km to reach a stile (at about GR 079893 on sheet 62) at a change in direction in a forest fence (the maps' borders and inaccuracy in the depiction of forests hereabouts make it difficult to work this out for yourself). It is important to reach this stile because a wide firebreak leads from it through an otherwise impenetrable sea of conifers. If you think you might miss it aim a little off in either direction and then walk in the appropriate direction to it. One other pointer: you should reach the stile just beyond a forest track (the one you were on earlier, in fact).

Follow the firebreak - and fence posts - gently upward. After about 20 minutes watch out for a clear firebreak on the left edged by dense arrays of trees. You will also note that the line of fence posts swings a little right at this point. Take this firebreak to a nearby forest track (it's the Wicklow Way again), turn right and follow it all the way down to the road at its crest (the Wicklow Way diverges to the right near the pass).

From here navigational problems are behind. Cross the road, pass through a gate on the other side and take a grassy track beyond towards the summit of Croaghanmoira. The track narrows to a path and then runs parallel to forest but the way is clear. Croaghanmoira (664m), on the edge of the mountains, commands wide views: small wonder that it was chosen as a primary triangulation point in the survey of the country.

From the summit diverge only slightly right from the upward path to climb its bland outlier 1km away to the north-west and then head north-east along the narrow, rocky Fananierin ridge, with good views to both left and right. As you approach its rocky summit you will cross a wall which will be useful for the return. From here to the summit is a there-and-back but worth the effort for the views along Glenmalure. By the way, don't be tempted to head north from Fananierin - it's *very* private. So, return to the wall, cross it, turn right downhill, veering away slightly from it to meet the end of a short stretch of track through forest and a useful bridge spanning Drumgoff Brook. This track leads shortly to the Military Road, from where it is downhill all the way to Drumgoff crossroads.

Variation from the South: If you are starting at Aghavannagh youth hostel (GR 0586) you can climb Croaghanmoira from there but be warned: there is much monotonous forest on the route. First arm yourself with sheet 62 or the Wicklow Way strip map (the former doesn't suffer from over-accuracy in its depiction of tracks). Walk to the Wicklow Way at GR 076850, take it generally uphill to leave the track and continue on a narrow path through trees (the waymark at the point where you leave the track is ambiguously placed). Where the Wicklow Way rejoins a track leave it to continue straight ahead roughly east following a path in a firebreak to emerge from forest near the summit of Croaghanmoira. Walk to the summit, descend to the crest of the road (at GR 0887), walk the road to the start. Walking time is 4.25 hours (distance 14km, climb 480m).

ROUTE 19: CARRIGLINEEN AND CULLENTRAGH

Good views over Glenmalure on the initial steep ascent of Carriglineen. Then a high route offering long-distance views and pleasant underfoot conditions, though with a little too much forest. An attractive section of the Wicklow Way, all on track, to finish.

Getting There: Drive to *Drumgoff crossroads* (GR 106909), turn left and park immediately in the carpark on the right.

Walking Time: 6 hours (distance 18km, climb 740m) including the climb to Kirikee (see below).

Difficulties: A fairly easy route navigationally, though the area round Mullacor is a little featureless and therefore may be difficult in bad visibility. The bracken to be waded through on the initial ascent might make this route unattractive in high summer (an alternative is given below).

Map: Sheet 56.

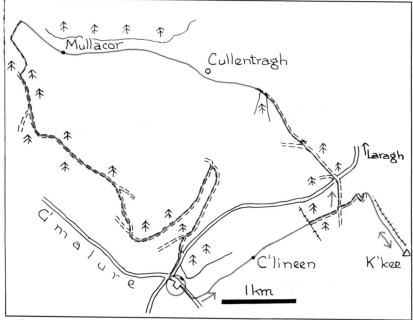

Route: Walk along the road away from the crossroads. Within the first few hundred metres you will find several places on the left to start the climb to Carriglineen. It doesn't matter exactly where you start but make sure you do not disturb sheep or cross fences unnecessarily and keep the edge of the forest some way off to the left (there's dreadful gorse near it). You will have to negotiate your way carefully what with gorse, bracken and the occasional rocky outcrop. The good views opening up over Glenmalure and far beyond may be some consolation. (The alternative to all this is to walk about 1km along the road from Drumgoff crossroads, here taking a side road on the left which ends high on the eastern side of Carriglineen.)

The summit of Carriglineen (455m) is crowned by an unpretentious cairn. After it continue north-east gently downhill on a developing path. About 1km from the summit you should cross a stile in a fence. Here the path improves to a good track and rough heather on both sides is augmented by, at the time of writing, tiny trees.

A few hundred metres beyond the stile you will reach a slightly off-set cross tracks and will have to decide whether to climb Kirikee or not (it doesn't add all that much to the delights of the route). If you want to, keep to the track running straight ahead and where it shortly expires after a few inconsequential wriggles, take the firebreak running south-east to the dumpy summit, which is crowned by a trig pillar. Return to the cross-tracks by the same route and turn right to reach the nearby highest point on the Military Road between Laragh and Drumgoff.

Cross the road to the forest entrance. The idea now is to walk straight ahead, that is north-west, ignoring tracks heading in other directions (they are shown on the sketch map). This will take you to a small wedge of mature trees on the left after about 1km, where you should cross a stile on the right and continue your north-westward progress, now on a path.

From here the inclination is nearly all steadily uphill right to the summit of Mullacor, on a rough path that gradually swings round to west and gives slowly expanding views. You will first pass the gentle mounds of the two summits of Cullentragh on the right, then you will see the rocky Derrybawn ridge off on the same side and shortly you will be walking parallel to a line of mature forest. Within 1km of the summit the slope eases, then the moderately steep slope resumes to the uninspiring summit plateau of short grass (4 hours).

At a lofty 657m Mullacor gives fairly good (not marvellous) views, particularly towards the Lugnaquillia massif to the south-west and along the Lugduffs ridge to the north-west, towards which we now head. Descend steeply the short distance to the col facing the Lugduffs and at a waymark there, turn left along the Wicklow Way. Follow it into forest on a muddy path, so reaching a track. From here on, depending on progress with tree-felling, there are good views down into Glenmalure and particularly across to Carrawaystick Waterfall, which cascades steeply into the valley. On a more practical level, there are several junctions ahead so it might not be a bad idea to concentrate on navigation, though mistakes will not be serious.

Turn left onto the track, keep straight ahead where the Wicklow Way heads right downhill, ignore a turn on the left, and fork left (maybe better described as straight ahead) at the next junction. This track swings left into the valley carrying the Military Road, descending only slightly as it does so. At the next junction, turn right steeply downhill to reach the road at Coolalingo Bridge, from where it is a short walk downhill to Drumgoff crossroads and the start.

ROUTE 20: CIRCUIT OF GLEN OW

A long walk with lovely views and fairly good underfoot, especially in the centre section, much of which is over 600m. However, it's a pity that there is so too much forestry to start. Unusually for Wicklow nearly all the climbing is before and all the descent after the highest point of the day, Lugnaquillia.

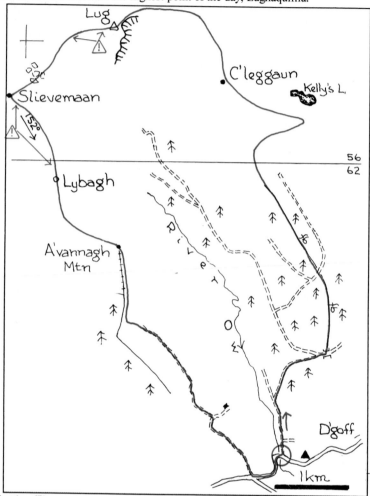

Getting There: A long 42 miles from Dublin, much of it over bad or indifferent roads. Drive to *Drumgoff crossroads,* continue south for nearly 6 miles, here forking right. Pass Aghavannagh youth hostel, park shortly beyond at the forestry entrance on the right (GR 055862).

Walking Time: 6.25 hours (distance 18km, climb 850m).

Difficulties: Navigation generally easy over mostly open country, though make sure that you descend the correct spur after Lugnaquillia. Do not attempt the walk in the opposite direction as this makes route finding much more difficult.

Map: Sheets 56 and 62. The transition from one to the other is easy. Forestry and forestry tracks are particularly badly shown on sheet 62, so the sketch map gives a little more detail than normal.

Route: Take the track at the forestry entrance and, ignoring a minor turn on the right which ends at a house, fork right after 700m or so. This takes you through a region of high trees with only the occasional view so it will be some consolation to reach a tee and the prospect of more interesting terrain.

At the tee turn right (alternatively it can be described as straight ahead) and almost immediately leave the track to take a wide firebreak running directly uphill and carrying a stream. Cross a forest track and continue onward and upward until you are into rough heather with forest a few hundred metres away on both sides.

Continue north-west on the crest of a broad, level spur. After crossing several fences in various stages of antiquity, you will come to a less decrepit fence marking the line of the highest forest. From here head north-east (the exact direction is luckily not vital, which is just as well because you are crossing the border from sheet 62 to 56). This will take you onto the high ground to the south of Kelly's Lough and to the start of the most memorable section of the walk.

Turn left when you reach the edge of steep ground plunging north towards the lough; there is no mistaking it. With the lake far below and the shoulder of Clohernagh beyond it, this is a lovely stretch whose scenery is sustained until well after Lugnaquillia, 3km to the west.

Corrigasleggaun (794m), crowned by a humble cairn, is the first peak to be climbed, after which there are renewed views of Kelly's Lough, now considerably further below. From Corrigasleggaun drop to the north-west and then resume the climb by joining another spur, that from Clohernagh, which comes in from the right.

As you face west towards Lugnaquillia, you are walking a gently sloping terrain of short grass, high above the bulk of the Wicklow mountains, with magnificent views in all directions. A general bearing west should suffice, though near the summit keep well clear of the South Prison (1), as it is easy enough to wander down when you encounter steep ground initially, though the cliffs nearer the summit are sheer and therefore unmistakable.

Lugnaquillia (925m, 3.75 hours) has a most unimpressive summit, an almost flat level plain of short grass, with a huge cairn at its centre. However walk only a few metres to north or south and the full majesty of your location immediately becomes apparent. To the north, overlooking the cliffs of the North Prison, is a wide panorama of mountains of which whale-backed Tonelagee is the most impressive. To east and west is high, unforested ground, while to the south, overlooking the South Prison, the mountains are lower, though the TV mast on Mount Leinster, the highest mountain in the Blackstairs, should be clearly visible in good weather. If in doubt as to the location of any feature you can refer to the mountain indicator a few metres from the cairn.

From the summit descend steep rock-strewn ground south-west - not west, where the enticing spur towards Camarahill beckons as one long continuous descent. The south-west descent ends in a flotilla of peat hags and wet ground from where Slievemaan (759m) is a short but stiff climb (you can circumvent the summit if you wish by passing it on its east side). The leg from Slievemaan passes back over onto sheet 62 with the not so inviting prospect of reaching a peak (Lybagh) with no discernible summit, not even a cairn. In bad weather take a compass bearing of about 152° for 1.5km to reach it; in good weather swing initially left of this bearing to keep to the high ground. The views along here are dramatic: unfortunately the best are behind you where the jaws of the South Prison yawn not altogether benignly.

The next peak, Aghavannagh Mountain (over 580m), is more accommodating navigationally, since a slight rise presages it and what is more, a line of fencing begins at the summit. Simply follow the fence downhill to a block of forest and follow the forest for a few hundred metres before veering away from it to reach a rough track (you can head directly for the track but you will encounter bog workings if you do).

Once on the track the rest is easy. Take it down through upland fields to another track, this one comparatively major, turn right onto it and follow it to tarmac at a tee. Turn left for the nearby start.

Escape/Shorter Variation: Admittedly not much of an escape route nor much shorter, but since it is in forest it may offer some shelter in bad weather. From the summit of Lugnaquillia descend steeply south with the cliffs of the South Prison close on the left (excellent views!) and so reach the corner of forest at GR 036906. Walk another few hundred metres south along the forest edge to a clear track heading into the forest. From here, with the help of the sketch map, you can easily find your way to the start.

Note

(1) The meaning of the names, the North and South Prisons, is obscure, with the popular explanation that they were 'prisons' for sheep being a trifle unlikely. However the origin of these impressive gougings into what are otherwise the bland, gently-sloping shoulders of Lugnaquillia is better known. Both Prisons are corries, where mountain glaciers were born during one of the ice ages. The accumulating snow, building up year after year, gouged out the corries and eventually flowed downhill as a glacier. The snow was more likely to accumulate on the sheltered north and east facing slopes and the South Prison is the only prominent corrie in these mountains that doesn't face north or east.

From the Spink (Routes 14, 15)

ROUTE 21: CIRCUIT OF UPPER GLENMALURE

Some spectacular views and locations to be savoured at the start and towards the end, but the centre section is over rough, tiring moorland with few interesting features near at hand, though the long views are good.

Getting There: Drive to *Drumgoff crossroads*, turn right and park in the large carpark at Baravore about 3 miles further on (GR 065942).

Walking Time: 5.75 hours (distance 16km, climb 840m) allowing about an extra 15 minutes for the initial steep ascent.

Difficulties: You can decide about the steep initial climb before you are committed to it and take the short variation if it looks too awe inspiring. There is a good deal of challenging navigation in one section offset by an escape route that is easy to find. In all, not the easiest of routes.

Map: Sheet 56.

Route: The initial section, which you can see by looking north-east across the road from the carpark, has a large vertical element to it. If you are not daunted climb directly from the road, picking an intermittent path through boulders, scree and high vegetation. After much effort you will reach one of several gullies hereabouts, which you might decide to climb through. Whether you do or not you can console yourself with the thought that these gullies mark the top of the steep ground and short grass making for easy progress lies above them.

When you reach this grass you certainly deserve a breather, during which you can admire the glorious Fraughan Rock Glen on the opposite side of Glenmalure and the cliffs of Ben Leagh overlooking them on the right .... of which more anon. You might also contemplate what you are going to do next. In good weather you might like to wander along the edge of steep ground north-west, aiming to reach eventually the high col between points 607m and 633m (GR 0596). In bad weather head directly for the crest of the Lugduff ridge (see also route 14) to reduce navigational problems.

At the col take the clear path to pt 633m and then continue in an arc to Conavalla over much wetter ground. (In bad weather omit Conavalla, an indistinct summit, and aim directly for Three Lakes.) Conavalla's summit is a plateau of pebbles, sand and the occasional peat hag. None too inspiring.

From Conavalla head over rough, wet ground to Three Lakes. You do not need to walk punctiliously to the lakeshore - it's very wet. Instead get within a few hundred metres of the lakes and then set your compass for Table Mountain to the south-west. This is a gentle climb over moorland that has a series of ditches cut into it which look man-made because they are straight and parallel to each other, but are presumably natural.

Table Mountain (701m) lives down to its name, with only a cairn to identify it. From the cairn push on south to an indistinct track, here at its highest point between Glenmalure and Glen of Imaal. If you miss it you should still find a signpost and a hollow close to it, the latter giving a little shelter. You are now 3.75 hours into the walk and can cut it short here by descending the track generally south-east directly back to the carpark.

From the hollow climb south to Camenabologue, on which stretch peat hags are accompanied by dry ground, an odd conjunction giving easy walking. Camenabologue (758m) has a good cairn and the views towards Lugnaquillia are magnificent. Descend initially south-east into boggy country and traverse an area of peat hags through which a path wanders. Keep on this path on part of the next rise, that towards pt 712m but at some convenient point veer east off the path to reach the eroded peat hags, some looking like giant mushrooms, which adorn the plateau summit of Ben Leagh (689m).

Walk east from Ben Leagh, keeping the crest of the spur slightly on the left to reach the edge of the nearby Ben Leagh cliffs, then turn left to walk the clear path along them. This is a lovely stretch; Fraughan Rock Glen far below, Art's Lough and the cliffs overlooking it beyond and a whole galaxy of lovely mountain country in all directions.

The path continues steeply downward through high heather to enter a difficult area where clumps of trees and felling makes for slow progress. Keep to the path if you can; otherwise you must struggle downward and north-eastward to a forest track, which isn't far away - in distance at least. At the track turn right to reach a nearby junction and continue downhill, looking out for a secluded, old path running acutely back on the right which offers a short cut through conifers (it doesn't matter too much if you miss it since you can continue down to the youth hostel and walk back from there). This path ends on tarmac opposite a footbridge. Cross the bridge and walk the few metres back to the carpark.

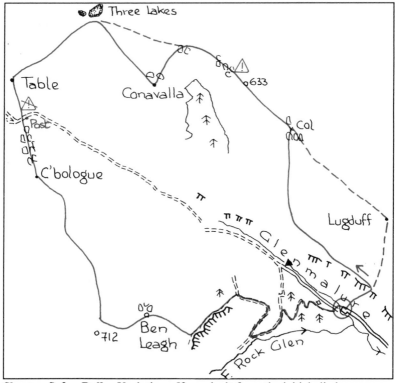

Shorter, Safer, Duller Variation: If you don't fancy the initial climb, you can cross the river at the carpark and walk north-west on road and track to the pass between Glenmalure and Glen of Imaal. Walk the rest of the route from there. Total walking time is 4.25 hours (distance 13km, climb 700m).

THE WEST

ROUTE 22: CIRCUIT OF GLENBRIDE

Starting at an exceptionally high level (370m), this walk reaches Mullagh-cleevaun, the second-highest peak in Wicklow on a good natural circuit. Before and after there is much open moorland with mercifully little afforestation.

Getting There: The start is about 30 miles from Dublin. Drive through *Blessington*, turn left onto the R758, pass through Valleymount, ignore the turn left towards Ballyknockan just beyond it, but fork left off the main road immediately after. Ignore the turn on the right, take the next turn left. Park near the bridge in the hamlet of Glenbride (GR 037042). You can also get to this point from the R756, generally a better road, but a longer route.

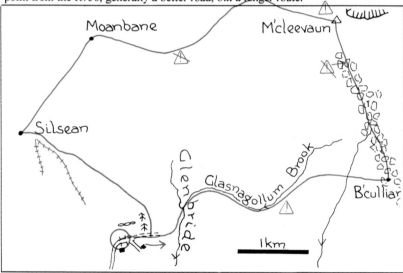

Walking Time: 4.5 hours (distance 12km, climb 640m).
Difficulties: Lots of very wet, boggy terrain and some minor ravines to negotiate south of Mullaghcleevaun. Generally difficult navigationally, though with no cliffs in the area, mistakes should not be costly.
Map: Sheet 56.
Route: Walk east from the bridge, shortly forking left to pass through a gate. Keep walking straight ahead along a track, or maybe it is merely a grassy area between fields. On this course you will begin to descend towards the main river in Glenbride, and since the general idea is to ascend, it is as well to veer left in order to cross the river a little upstream. As you approach the river, look out for Glassnagollum Brook, which is marked by a deep trench slicing through bogland and is your route towards Barnacullian.

The Brook may be followed uphill until its course swings decisively from south-east to north-east, or rather would if it were flowing uphill. Keep along it for a while longer and then, in good visibility anyway, you might try to find Barnacullian, a metal post in an ocean of eroded hags. To do this swing east from the Brook onto gently shelving moorland, cross one major stream, and continue to slog onward, firmly dismissing unworthy thoughts about needles in haystacks. (In poor visibility it might be as well to follow the bank of the Brook to its source and from there head directly to the summit of Mullaghcleevaun.)

From Barnacullian the aim is to reach Mullaghcleevaun. Keep to the high ground to face the most notorious part of the notorious Barnacullian ridge. The ground directly south of Mullaghcleevaun is riven with steep-sided ravines, some several metres deep. Since these are obviously difficult to cross, you can expect slow progress along here. At length the ground steepens, the ravines are left behind and there is only the final fairly short climb to the summit.

Mullaghcleevaun (847m, 3 hours) has a trig pillar that serves as a focus to its summit plateau. Just to its north, overlooking the corrie containing Cleevaun Lough is a memorial to three An Oige members drowned in a boating accident in the fifties. The views are not quite as good as one would expect from this lofty location, the tenth highest mountain in Ireland. Three high spurs running south, north-east and west dominate the scene, with impressive Tonelagee prominent beyond the end of the Barnacullian ridge to the south. Beyond and between these spurs is a wide panorama of scenic hills. Overall, a worthy goal for the day.

The route from Mullaghcleevaun is difficult in bad weather. Descend steeply westward (exactly 295° compass) at first, but after 1.5km from the summit (18 minutes or so) swing left to keep to high ground; there is nothing to indicate exactly where to turn, but if you hit a distinct area of peat hags you are a little too far north. The aim here is to reach Moanbane (703m), a gently rounded peak offering good views over Pollaphuca Reservoir (as indeed does Silsean, the next peak). A north-south oriented lake about 7 double-steps across marks the summit, with nothing much else of note. From here head south-west, dipping 30m and rising even less to reach the modest summit of Silsean (698m).

Silsean's summit plateau is very similar to Moanbane's, the main difference being that the summit plateau has a flotilla of lakes. More important for navigation is the acute junction of two fences just to the east off the summit plateau - the trees indicated on sheet 56, which the fence presumably should bound, have not been planted.

Walk to this junction and keep the fences on the right. As you descend veer away from the fences to keep to the crest of a south-east running spur. Beyond it civilisation emerges in the form of upland fields edged by a line of conifers. Keep these trees on the right to meet the indistinct track on which you started and turn right onto it for the nearby start.

ROUTE 23: SORREL HILL TO BALLYKNOCKAN

The road which runs along the eastern shore of Pollaphuca Reservoir is lined with farmland and can be penetrated in only a few places. The main route therefore is an A to B requiring two cars. It traverses muted peaks which offer good views west over the reservoir and towards more distinctive mountain country in other directionns.

Getting There: Drive both cars through *Lackan* and park one just before the village of Ballyknockan in the large carpark on the left (GR 010073). Drive the second car back through Lackan and park 1½ miles beyond the village on waste ground on the left opposite a cul de sac sign (GR 993124).

Walking Time: 5.75 hours (distance 17km, climb 780m).

Difficulties: Unless you are quite confident (and able) don't attempt this route in bad visibility as there is a good chance of getting lost. Lots of wet ground and more important, some difficult navigation in the centre section. However in an emergency you can always head directly west to the road.

Map: Sheet 56.

Route: Walk up the cul de sac road to the corner of forest and fork left to take the forest track. Turn left off the track at the first clear firebreak - it doesn't matter if you miss it as there are several clear passages. Cross two tracks to emerge on the crest of the spur named Lugnagun.

Once there, turn right to face Sorrel Hill. This is a pleasant, easy stretch: good ground underfoot, forest and later an earthbank on the right to take care of navigational worries, and fairly good views in all directions.

The earthbank continues onto the lower slopes of Sorrel, after which the climb to the summit is easy. Sorrel (599m) is crowned by a huge cairn on an eroded area of rock and sand. The views are good: Seahan and Seefingan to the north-east with a whole line of gently moulded peaks of which the highest is Mullaghcleevaun on the southern horizon.

It is this direction which we must now face. Descend south to reach a minor road and carpark at Ballynultagh Gap, from where take the bog road southwards to its end near the summit of Black Hill (602m, 3.25 hours). Walk the remaining distance to the summit, an unshapely upturned pudding bowl.

Navigation from here on is quite difficult on gently sloping, featureless terrain and with turning points in the middle of nowhere. In good weather you can descend south-east from Black Hill, skirt round the soggy headwaters of Ballynastockan Brook and then climb the bland shoulder of Moanbane. In bad visibility (and let's hope you aren't there in such conditions), a compass bearing directly from Black Hill to Billy Byrne's Gap (at GR 0406) might be the best bet; you will notice the steady if unspectacular drop into Glenbride if you begin to overshoot it.

Once at the Gap you can begin the steady climb to the summit plateau of Moanbane (703m) to the west, where a north-south oriented lake about 7 double-steps across marks the summit, an admittedly meagre landmark. The next target is Silsean (698m), Moanbane's more or less twin sister and no more notable than Moanbane. On this summit plateau, or rather just to its east is a useful landmark: an acute junction of two fences.

From Silsean descend directly north-west and when, far down the slope you encounter forest (not shown on the current sheet 56) keep it on the right to reach a gate with a road beyond it and beyond that again the untidy quarry workings. Take this road down to the village, ignoring lots of side roads ending at houses or the quarry. In the village turn right, take the immediate turn on the right and walk directly back to the car park.

One Car Variation: Take the main route to the summit of Black Hill, descend west to pick up a grassy track. Turn right onto it to reach a large complex of buildings surrounded by a rectangular fringe of trees. Turn right to walk round one side of this fringe, then head north to the road. Turn left here, keep on the road for a few hundred metres, then fork right to climb gently across open country and cross a gate at a forest edge about 100m from its lower end. Take the left branch at a hairpin bend at the gate, walk directly to the start. Total walking time is 5.5 hours (distance 17km, climb 660m).

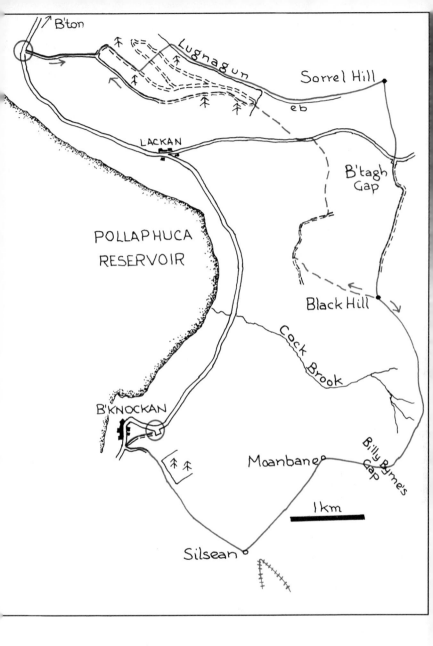

B'ton

Lugnagun

Sorrel Hill

eb

LACKAN

B'tagh
Gap

POLLAPHUCA
RESERVOIR

Black Hill

Cock Brook

B'KNOCKAN

Billy Byrne's
Gap

Moanbane

1km

Silsean

ROUTE 24: FAIR MOUNTAIN AND LOUGH FIRRIB

Some of the bleakest territory in Wicklow, with much undulating moorland and many areas of peat hag. Yet on a fine day this can be an enjoyable route with long and varied views and the satisfaction of finding your way round a circuit featuring only a few distinct landmarks.

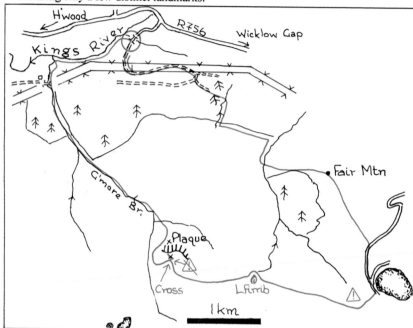

Getting There: From Dublin (about 33 miles) it's probably marginally easier to get there from the west than the east. Drive through *Blessington*, continue on the N81 to turn left onto the R756. Continue straight ahead for another 7 miles to cross the prominent Ballinagee Bridge. Take the nearby next turn right, the first for miles, and park near the first (and only) bridge (GR 033019).

Walking Time: 4.5 hours (distance 14km, climb 560m).

Difficulties: Lots of wet ground and much compass work needed. Although there are no cliffs in the area, King's River and the great expanses of forestry plantations bounding the R756 do not allow an easy escape if you get lost.

Map: Sheet 56. Some forest tracks and a vital firebreak are not shown.

Route: Take the track running south from the bridge, ignoring initially the minor fork left. Where it starts to swing in a hairpin to the right directly under the pylons look out for a path on the left running gently downhill and starting just after passing under the second set of pylons. That's not the path you want! Instead walk a few more metres to where the track swings decisively right and take a muddy path on the left heading gently upward.

This path lasts for only about 5 minutes' walking and when it peters out continue straight ahead (make sure it is straight ahead) through a stretch of forest on an intermittent path. At the forestry fence, reached in 2 minutes or so from entering forest, turn right to follow a narrow stream, mature trees on the right, younger trees on the left. Pass a rocky outcrop, unusual in this area, and cross another fence to reach open country.

You are now on the spur running north from Oakwood (at about GR 042009), with the next goal Fair Mountain (569m, GR 0600) to the east. Keep the fence close on the left and walk about 1km to reach a stream set in a tiny, charming valley beyond which the rocky northern flank of Fair Mountain looms close at hand. It's pleasant to walk a little upstream (maybe a few hundred metres) before tackling this steep hillside - it also postpones a strenuous climb

Leave the stream to climb directly to the summit, a most unimpressive affair since Fair Mountain is only a spur reaching north-west from Turlough Hill. The huge standing boulders on the way up and on the summit itself are the only notable features. You can't miss Turlough Hill! The mighty ramparts bordering the Upper Reservoir are all too visible from all around. Walk towards it, picking up a tarmac road on the way, to reach a plateau close to the Upper Reservoir. From there walk south-west a few hundred metres to the disused met station.

Lough Firrib is next. A tiny lake which you will probably not see until you are upon it because of the undulating moorland around, it demands careful navigation even in good weather. There is an intermittent set of bootmarks across the moorland to the lake but careful compass work is still required.

Lough Firrib's shore (3 hours) is a good place for a rest and a think about how to reach Art's Cross (GR 038990), which is actually set vertically and constructed of two sturdy wooden beams at right angles - yes, the real thing. In bad visibility perhaps the best bet is to start off on a compass bearing of 294° and then to veer gradually left from this to avoid steep ground. Since it is only a little more than 1km from Lough Firrib it should not be too difficult to find.

From Art's Cross there are several choices (see below). For the main route walk a little west to avoid crags and then descend directly to the upper end of Glenreemore, a tiny pocket of flat land. Here, set into the rocks at the foot of slabs you might chance upon Art's Plaque. The stretch from this pocket is easy navigationally and a delight to walk, a remote and wild area with fine, bold hillsides rising on both sides. Cross Glenreemore Brook early on to avoid a difficult fording later, then walk north-west along its bank to descend through a wide, clear space between two forestry plantations.

Eventually you will come to a bridge spanning the now formidable Brook. Do not cross it. Instead, keep the river close on your left and follow it resolutely downstream on a narrow path edged by trees. After a few minutes you will notice that the river has seemingly changed direction: you are now walking upstream. The explanation is that you have passed the hidden junction of Glenreemore Brook and King's River and are now on the banks of the latter.

From here on it is easy navigationally and a lovely, scenic walk in spite of the uneven path. Simply keep the river on the left: you may have to detour from it a little here and there to avoid dense trees. The last few hundred metres is in open country so you are unlikely to miss the bridge where you started.

Minor Variations: From Art's Cross walk 200m or so west to descend a spur northwards. Remember that this will mean crossing Glenreemore Brook further downstream and that might be difficult. More ambitiously, you can walk to Three Lakes, where there are *two* lakes plonked in a desolate area and from there follow the Asbawn Brook down, taking care to circumvent one section of cliff just to the north of Three Lakes. Again, remember you have to cross Glenreemore Brook.

ROUTE 25: MULLAGHCLEEVAUN FROM THE NORTH

An area of abundant gently sloping moorland is not at first glance an inviting one. However the scenic high ground of the centre section of the route is preceded by a walk along the banks of a stream slicing through that moorland, thus making a surprisingly varied route.

Getting There: From Dublin there are two possible routes. The shorter is to take the N81 towards *Blessington*, turn left off it onto the R759 just after Brittas, follow signs for Sally Gap for over 4 miles to turn right (signed 'Blessington 6') to cross the River Liffey. Turn first left (set your milometer here), ignore the cul-de-sac road on the left and drive to the forest entrance 2.1 miles from the tee (the second of two closely spaced entrances on the left) (GR 058118). The road is extremely narrow for the last few miles.

The alternative is to drive to *Lackan,* fork left here towards Ballynultagh Gap where there is a carpark (GR 044108). You should start the commentary at the last paragraph below.

Walking Time: 5.5 hours (distance 16km, climb 580m), which allows some time for slow progress along a river bank.

Difficulties: Near the start a river to ford which may be difficult after rain, soft ground in many places and a few points where careful navigation is required.

Map: Sheet 56.

Route: Take the narrow road into forest (not the forest track on its right). Emerging from forest at a tee, take the left branch and just before the 'temporary' dwelling, beyond which is a farmhouse, turn right off the track and head generally south through abandoned fields to reach Ballydonnell Brook, the main stream in the valley, on the left.

Shortly after reaching the Brook you should come to a fence corner beyond which are young trees. From this corner walk upstream for another few minutes until you come to a major tributary (it's Lugaculleen Brook). Cross Ballydonnell Brook here (you may have to go some distance upstream) and follow Lugaculleen Brook to its source, which it does without gathering any major tributary, a fact which greatly simplifies navigation. You will pass some deciduous trees on the south-west bank at a narrow cleft shortly after leaving Ballydonnell Brook; otherwise there are no major features until you come to an area that looks like a field, with steep, rocky slopes rising behind it at about GR 084085. The steep, rocky, slopes are real enough, but the 'field' is only a reedy low-lying area.

From the 'field' climb steeply south-east to the left of scattered crags and so reach high ground, Duff Hill to the east, Mullaghcleevaun East Top to the south-west and, at this point only of academic interest, the rim of the corrie holding Cleevaun Lough the main feature to the west.

The East Top is the next goal. Note that it has two tops, both to be climbed: the first has a cairn on a boulder, the higher top (795m) to the south-west has a cairn on flat ground with lots of tastefully disposed boulders scattered around it. From East Top the climb to Mullaghcleevaun is easy, though you may want to swing right of the direct line to avoid a slough of black mud in the shallow col.

Mullaghcleevaun (847m, 3.25 hours), (briefly described under route 22) has a trig pillar which makes it unmistakable. From the summit it's worthwhile walking north to the corrie edge to look down into Cleevaun Lough.

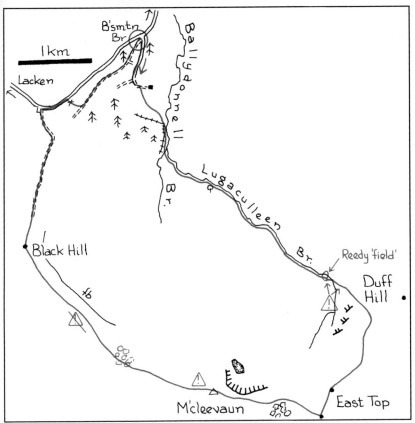

The next stretch as far as Black Hill nearly 4km away is one of the most featureless in Wicklow. This means attention to navigation, though there are no hazards apart from the initial cliffs over the Cleevaun Lough corrie. From Mullaghcleevaun summit head west (exactly 300° compass) steeply downhill to cross a compact and distinct region of hags, and so of some help in navigation. Then, keeping a broad firebreak off to the right, cross a soggy plain and ascend the soggy slopes of Black Hill to finally arrive at its soggy summit (602m).

With sogginess now thankfully behind walk north from Black Hill to pick up a bog track. This takes you to the carpark at Ballynultagh Gap. From the Gap turn right to walk along the road, crossing the first gate on the right after a few hundred metres. Take the wide grassy firebreak beyond through scattered trees to a forest track. Turn left onto it and walk the kilometre or so straight back to the start.

ROUTE 26: SOUTH OF THE KING'S RIVER

A region of indistinct peaks, several small lakes set in rolling moorland and few other landmarks make for a walk which is difficult but satisfying to navigate. Long views over more distinct mountains, the expanse of Pollaphuca Reservoir and the plains of Kildare compensate for unvarying ground underfoot. A short route but one which can easily be extended (see below).

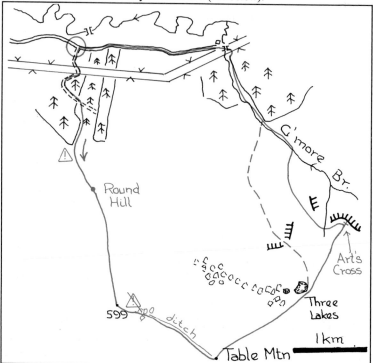

Getting There: Take the N81 past *Blessington*, turn left onto the R756, drive for just over 3 miles, here continuing straight ahead where the main road swings sharply left. Park at the forest entrance on the right 2.4 miles along this road (GR 001014). The total distance from central Dublin is about 31 miles.

Walking Time: 4.25 hours (distance 13km, climb 540m).

Difficulties: As indicated above, navigation is the main difficulty. The consolation is that there are few dangerous areas in the vicinity so a compass bearing north will probably take you to (or close to) a gap in blocks of forest reaching north to King's River.

Map: Sheet 56. The full length of the initial track is not shown.

Route: From the forest entrance take the track and where it emerges from mature trees into an area of young ones, leave it to walk upward through new forest, mature forest on the right. On reaching the southern end of two blocks of mature forest, one on each side, head directly south to nearby Round Hill (511m), which is simply a small but reassuring cairn in an area where there are no others.

From here on navigation is difficult. The route given here takes in all the small (but distinct) landmarks around and so makes navigation as easy as possible, an especially important point in bad visibility. However this is a route which allows much scope for improvisation, so there's plenty of choice in good weather.

From Round Hill head over moorland to pt 599m to the south, notable only because the gentle slope upward yields to an equally gentle slope downward. From here head east for only a few hundred metres to the point (at GR 009979) where there is a distinct area of peat hags and a wide and clear ditch heading south-east to Table Mountain (701m). Follow this ditch nearly to the 'summit' of Table, if the stony plateau can be dignified as such. However it does have a substantial cairn, so you are unlikely to miss it.

From Table a compass bearing (61°) on Three Lakes about 1.5km away over undulating moorland might be prudent. This being Ireland there are only *two* lakes; they are set on a wind-swept soggy plateau and are probably the most uninviting small mountain lakes in the range. From here head directly for Art's Cross (GR 038990), which is a vertical assemblage and so visible for miles around, except in bad visibility when you really need it.

As stated under route 24 there are a variety of descents from Art's Cross. For the present route let's walk north along the high spur to the west of Glenreemore Brook keeping initially to the right of the crest to enjoy the sight of the occasional crags overlooking Glenreemore. As you do so gradually work your way down to the valley floor so you can cross the Brook before it becomes unfordable.

Once across the Brook follow it downhill to be funnelled into an unplanted area between two blocks of forest. After passing under the pylons cross a rough bridge, turn left to follow a gradually improving track (you will note that there's plenty of room for improvement) all the way back to the start about 2km away.

ROUTE 27: KEADEEN AND SLIEVEMAAN

A walk without a convincing unity. Keadeen, a bulky but none too shapely peak, stands a little aloof from the rest of the range and does not make a sufficiently long one-day walk on its own. To lengthen it an outlier of Lugnaquillia can be climbed and the narrow sliver of lowland separating Keadeen from the rest of the range crossed twice.

Getting There: The total distance from central Dublin is about 38 miles. There are several ways of getting to the start, none of them easy. One way is to drive to *Donard*, continue onward past the youth hostel, shortly after turn first right to Knockanarrigan, continue straight ahead in that village, fork first right over a bridge to keep on the main road, turn left immediately to pass Dwyer's Cottage, fork first right and park at the forest entrance (and bridge) where forest ceases on the right but not on the left (GR 984895) (phew!). There is room here for several (only several) carefully parked cars.

Walking Time: 6.5 hours (distance 19km, climb 900m).

Difficulties: Some navigational uncertainty in farmland especially on the descent from Carrig and the ascent to Slievemaan, but no dangerous terrain anywhere in the area.

Maps: Sheets 56 and 62.

Route: Take the track from the forest entrance, and after a few metres, you will come to a hairpin bend in a major track. Don't take either leg; instead take the rutted, grassy track on the left heading back to the forest edge. At this edge walk steadily upward to the higher edge of the forest and then follow a rutted track heading directly to the summit. Good views reveal themselves slowly as you ascend, that to the Lugnaquillia massif (unfortunately behind) being particularly impressive.

Instead of following this track all the way to near the summit, you might consider veering to the right off it to get a better view of the Glen of Imaal (1). It's a peaceful agricultural oasis with a surprisingly large area under trees to break up the field pattern.

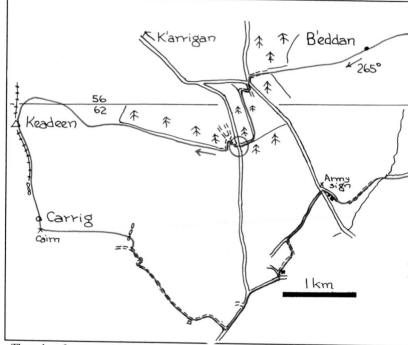

There is a fence running north-south along the summit ridge, so a turn left at it will take you to the huge heap of stones (and a trig pillar) on the summit. (The OS have designated these stones as a 'cairn'; they have also dignified several other much less impressive mounds in this area as being of archaeological significance.)

The views stretch out from Keadeen (653m) west towards the plains of Kildare and beyond. One feature that you might look out for are the walls circling lop-sidedly Brusselstown Ring to the west: the summit of Keadeen must be the one point from which you can appreciate their full magnitude.

But onward. Walk south from Keadeen following the fence, and at the col facing Carrig keep on south, now following a wall which persists for only a hundred metres or so on the climb. Indeed Carrig (571m) is hardly worth even the short climb; however the cairn just south of the vague summit does leave you in a good position to reach the lowlands.

Walk from the summit along the south (right) side of the grassy spur reaching east from Carrig, cross the first wall beyond which the land rises in upland fields, turn right immediately and walk down to the nearby track. Turn left to follow the track south-east. Here and there it degenerates to parallel lines of stone walls, so the first ruin you reach might be reassuring because there is a distinct track just beyond it. To reach it keep the ruin on the right and walk it to gain the nearby road (2.75 hours) and the nearby car, if you are so inclined.

Considerable road and track follows, mostly narrow and traffic-free. Briefly described: turn left onto the road, walk past Honey Bee Farm (great name!), turn right just beyond it, first left, keep straight ahead onto a track, turn right onto tarmac again and walk straight ahead to an Army sign. Here (at GR 996888) continue straight ahead on a track flanked by an irregular line of houses.

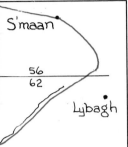

Turn left off this track somewhere opposite the first or second houses, and walk up through one (only) narrow field bordered by huge stone walls. Cross the wall at the end of the field, taking care not to dislodge stones, then turn half-right and gently uphill to reach a track running parallel to Derreen River down on the right. The track quickly peters out, though not as quickly as the path which replaces it. Around here descend gradually to the river (you should be close to a major confluence) and take the right branch upstream.

From here all is easy for some time, at least navigationally. Simply follow the stream to its source high on the spur between Slievemaan and Lybagh, walking all the while through a vast gently sloping plain of rough grass, to which the stream offers much-needed diversification. Having gained the crest of the spur walk north-west to Slievemaan (it doesn't help that you are right on the maps' borders). The summit offers a superb viewpoint, with the great block of Lugnaquillia particularly impressive. From here walk west to a rocky outcrop just before the col facing Ballineddan and from there ascend over short grass to the summit (652m).

There is a clear path from Ballineddan. Don't take it! Instead, on a compass bearing of 265° walk downhill through the occasional band of rock to reach a broad firebreak carrying a track and ending on tarmac. Turn left here to a nearby junction. Continue straight ahead on a rough track through young trees, turn right at the nearby tee and walk to the border between mature and young trees. Turn left to follow the border of the mature trees until barred by forest ahead. Turn right here up a firebreak to reach a bridge, the bridge at which you started.

Variations: As you can see from the sketch map it is easy to climb Keadeen and Carrig only. It's also easy to climb Slievemaan and Ballineddan only though in this case it is well worthwhile to tackle Lugnaquillia from Slievemaan.

Note

(1) No plague in the Glen. A few years ago, I wrote an article about this area for a British walking magazine and made the unfortunate error of referring to the 'bubonic peace' of the Glen, and not the 'bucolic peace' that I intended. The incorrect version duly appeared in the magazine. I am pleased to confirm that if peace reigns in the Glen it is not because all the inhabitants have died of the plague.

ROUTE 28: CHURCH MOUNTAIN AND LOBAWN

Good but not spectacular long-range views over much of the route offsets the dull gently sloping terrain underfoot. The present abundance of conifers covering the lower slopes of the hills is poised to extend further.

Getting There: Drive to *Donard* (GR 9397) and park in the village.

Walking Time: 5.25 hours (distance 16km, climb 700m).

Difficulties: The main difficulty is to circumnavigate forestry though with no dangerous areas in the area, a modicum of care should see you through.

Map: Sheet 56.

Route: From the village take the road north, that is so that you shortly pass the RC Church. Continue onward, cross Hell Kettle Bridge and turn right just after to walk up a narrow road edged by high hedges which unfortunately block the views. Pass the last farm on the road and now on a track, walk a few further metres, here turning off left onto rough ground on the southern slopes of Church.

The walk from here to the summit is easy, a gentle ascent all the way. First cross a fence with a short stretch of forest beyond and then keep to the left of new forest that reaches to just east of the summit and will prove useful on the descent. Church (544m) is crowned by heaps of stones plus a trig pillar. The views in all directions are particularly good, with the three highest peaks in Wicklow - Lugnaquillia, Mullaghcleevaun and Tonelagee - all clearly visible on a good day. As well as all this, there is the prospect over the sprawling Pollaphuca Reservoir.

The descent requires some care if you are not to be ensnared in new forestry. Perhaps the best plan is to walk the few metres east to the forestry fence, turn left and walk to a fence corner from where a clear firebreak cum ditch leads downhill, young trees on the right, mature ones on the left. Follow it to nearly level ground at the col between Church and Corriebracks, here veering right to follow an old track to a wider, clearer one. Turn left onto it to pass through a nearby substantial gate. From about here incidentally, a backward glance encompasses the corduroy-like patches of drainage channels adorning the slopes of Church. Not a pretty sight.

Take the main track gently upward, forest close on the right. Keep on the track as it veers away from this forest and fork right where a solitary conifer is prominent off to the left. Shortly after the track ends, but the 'summit' of Corriebracks (531m) is only a few metres further south, that is if you can find it, because it is a virtual plateau.

From Corriebracks continue south, shortly crossing a fence, a useful indication that you have in fact passed the summit. From here to the western spur of Lobawn 2km to the south the route is easy: simply keep forest on the right. Just before you reach the lowest point on this stretch note the gap in the forest on the right, a useful escape route. There is a stiff climb to the crest of the spur but the views from here make it well worth it: Glen of Imaal at your feet and the great Lugnaquillia massif further off with the North Prison prominent.

Follow the wide but intermittent ditch east to the summit of Lobawn (636m), which is marked by a 'WD' pillar. This stands for war department - nowadays there is of course no such department, only defence being appropriate. The views are an extension of what you have already seen with in addition, a large chunk of mountain country off to the east.

At Lobawn (with about 1.5 hours' walking of the main route still to do) you have to make a decision whether to continue on this route or to take the slightly longer variation, described below. If you want to stay with the main route, retrace your steps west along the ditch until it expires and then follow a fence running in the same direction. When you reach a scattered pile of stones pick up a track running downhill into a pleasant landscape of upland fields. The track eventually reaches forest on the left and a gate a little further on. Cross it and turn right to reach a farmhouse and farmyard on the right.

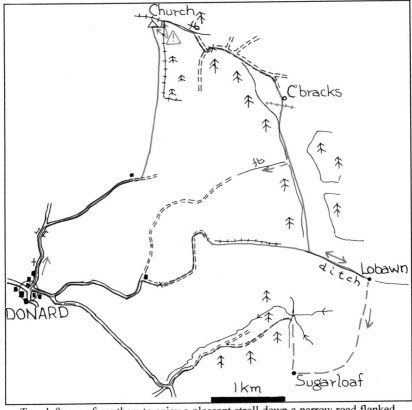

Turn left away from them to enjoy a pleasant stroll down a narrow road flanked by trees. At the main road, or at least the relatively main road, turn right to reach the village a few hundred metres on.

Longer Variation: This variation has the advantage that you remain at a high level for longer than on the main route and so the views are that much better. The disadvantage is that you face nearly 3km of road walk at the end. The extra walking time is about a half-hour.

From Lobawn walk south and then west to the summit of Sugarloaf, an almost level stretch. Descend north to a deep, narrow valley, crossing a stile on the left into forestry land just before you reach the valley's stream. All the while walking south-west, take the intermittent path beyond, which improves to a track and then to a minor road. Turn right onto the main road near Snugborough Bridge and walk from there into Donard.

ROUTE 29: LUGNAQUILLIA AND THE UPPER GLEN OF IMAAL

A long and lovely walk, much of it over high ground with expansive views over impressive mountain scenery. Underfoot conditions are generally good. Because of the proximity of the Artillery Range not a route that can be easily shortened.

Getting There: Drive to *Donard*, continue straight ahead past the youth hostel. About 1.6 miles beyond it park at the forest entrance on the left with a junction opposite it. There is ample space here for carefully parked cars (GR 983948). You can also park at Fenton's pub further south (GR 973935).

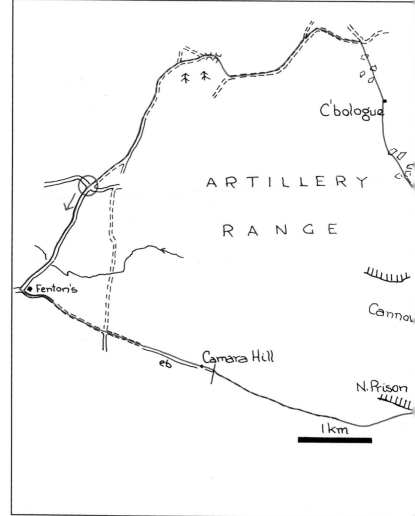

Walking Time: 6.25 hours (distance 19km, climb 900m).

Difficulties: There are paths for most of the way but do not rely on them to do the navigation for you. In particular, careful navigation is required on the descent from Lugnaquillia. Except in an emergency, you are committed to the route from beyond its summit because of the need to keep clear of the Artillery Range. Note that though the route passes through the Range (as shown on the OS map) it is still approved unless red flags are flying on the approach roads. If they are you will have to take the slightly longer public road alternative.

Map: Sheet 56.

Route: Take the road south (that is, right from the direction on which you drove) for less than 2km to pass Fenton's pub. Turn left just beyond it and walk onward over an extremely rutted road, which soon becomes a track complete with formidable pools of water. At a cross tracks continue straight ahead on a grassy track running up the face of Camarahill. Note that you can also reach this cross tracks by walking onward from the start and turning right onto a narrow road after 200m or so - but only when red flags are not flying.

This track lasts for only a few hundred metres, but an earthbank will guide you all the way to the summit (480m) and beyond it for 100m or so on a short downhill, the one and only this side of Lug. Pass a heap of rocks and then start the climb to Lugnaquillia in earnest on a rough but continuous path.

This is a lovely stretch, the cliffs of the North Prison ahead, the Ballineddan spur approaching from the right and the great unforested expanse of the Artillery Range down on the left. Navigation is easy: just follow the rough path which runs generally east to expire temporarily at steeper boulder-strewn ground close to Lug. On the summit plateau the slope relents and the path resumes over short grass to the great summit cairn itself.

Lugnaquillia (925m, 3.25 hours) is described under route 17. Suffice to say here that it commands a marvellous view over a vast array of mountain scenery.

The descent requires a little care, the general idea being to reach the summit of Camenabologue (GR 0295) 4km to the north. From Lug take a bearing of 50° compass for 400m and then swing to 326° for about 800m, taking care at the end of this leg not to walk too far onto the beguiling grassy shoulder of Cannow. Instead swing right, keeping to the high ground and picking up a prominent path which will ensure that you do not wander east onto the plentiful peat hags on Benleagh (689m) and pt 663m.

The path leads down a rocky spur with a whole galaxy of peaks ahead: the great hump of Tonelagee beyond the pumped storage reservoir, muted Mullaghcleevaun further away to its left and even the tip of the Great Sugar Loaf. And not only peaks, for there are marvellous views into Glenmalure and beyond Fraughan Rock Glen to lofty Art's Lough, tucked in under the cliffs of Clohernagh.

The lower ground just south of Camenabologue is soggy and has peat hags, after which there is a steep and unmistakable climb of about 150m to the summit (758m), crowned by an imposing cairn in a boulder field. This is the first major cairn since Lug and therefore of some use in bad visibility. From Camenabologue it is a short and pleasant walk downhill through the occasional peat hag to the top of the pass (at GR 0296) between Glen of Imaal and Glenmalure, which offers a sheltered little nook for grub.

The rest of the route, waymarked path or track all the way, is that approved by the Army authorities and is easy to describe and indeed walk. Sadly, after the splendours of the route so far, it is a little monotonous. From the pass start off downhill to the west, taking not the better grassy track running north-west but the initially more modest indistinct track on its left. Continue downhill until Army waymarks divert you right off the track, past skeletons of trees on the left and across two adjacent footbridges. These lead to a nearby forest track, later a rutted road, which should be followed until you are diverted right off this back onto a forest track for the last few hundred metres.

A Completely Different Variation: A shorter walk, and though with lovely scenery not quite as varied as the main route. Park at Fenton's (see above). Take the above route to Lugnaquillia, then head south-west on a navigationally simple stretch to Slievemaan and Ballineddan. Follow route 27 to the road (at GR 986903). Turn right and if the Army flags are not flying you can walk directly to the junction at the foot of Camarahill, which you will recognise from earlier in the day. Turn left here for Fenton's. Walking time is 5.5 hours (distance 16km, climb 850m).

Lugnaquillia and the North Prison (Route 29) -

APPROACHES TO THE LUGNAQUILLIA MASSIF

As the highest mountain in Ireland outside Kerry (a significant qualification!) Lugnaquillia (925m) is the goal for large numbers of walkers, especially as it stands at the apex of an expansive area of highly scenic hill country.

The following brief summary of the most popular approaches to the mountain partly duplicates information given in some of the routes. The approaches are given in a clockwise direction starting at the north.

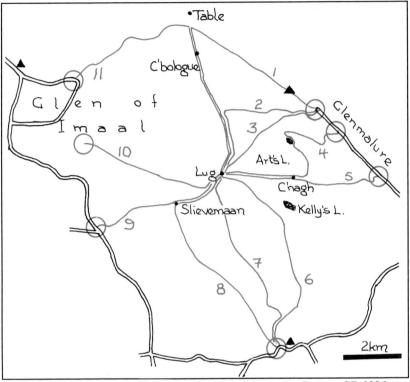

1. Baravore carpark (GR 0694) → Track north-west to Pass-at GR 0296 → Camenabologue. A long slog from the carpark, partly through forest ends at the pass at GR 0296 in open, highly scenic country with wide views. One of the longest approaches to Lug (walking time for ascent 4.25 hours, descent 3 hours).

2. Baravore carpark → Ben Leagh-→ Col at GR 0394 (see also route 21). A lovely stretch along the tops of the Ben Leagh cliffs and then into the open country of the last approach. It is advisable to tackle this route from Lug first as the path north of Ben Leagh is difficult to find from the Baravore direction and the underfoot conditions if not found very treacherous. (3.25 hours up, 2 hours down.)

3. Baravore → Fraughan Rock Glen (see also route 17). A dramatic, lovely approach into the Glen with cliffs on both sides for part of the way and even an accompanying cascade. The shortest and probably the best of all the approaches to Lug. (2.75 hours up; 1.5 hours down so allowing extra time for a steep descent.)

4. Glenmalure (GR 079928) → Art's Lough → Clohernagh (see also route 17). A forest track ends close to the shores of Art's Lough. From here take a grassy ramp south-east to climb Clohernagh and continue through highly scenic country. (3.25 hours up, 2 hours down.)

5. Glenmalure (GR 087922). ➔ Clohernagh. A zig-zag track starting close to a farmhouse *(do not disturb the residents)* ends on level ground east of Clohernagh, with a lovely walk to the summit. Note that the tracks shown on sheet 56 in the upper valley of the Carrawaystick Brook do not exist. (3 hours up, 1.75 hours down.)

6. Aghavannagh (GR 055862) ➔ Spur South of Corrigasleggaun (see also route 20). Rather too much forest to start followed by lovely views over Kelly's Lough. If attempting this route from Lug veer left off the crest of the spur south of Corrigasleggaun to reach a forest track and so avoid becoming entangled in forest. (3.5 hours up, 2.25 hours down.)

7. Aghavannagh (GR 055862). ➔ Forest Tracks ➔ South Prison (see also route 20). Far too much forest track (these are correctly shown on sheet 62) ends just south of the summit with a steep ascent close to the South Prison. (3.25 hours up, 2 hours down.)

8. Aghavannagh (GR 055862) ➔ Lybagh ➔ Slievemaan (see also route 20). A gradual ascent through open, gently sloped mountains giving excellent views of the South Prison. (4 hours up, 2.5 hours down.)

9. Ballinfoyle (GR 986913). ➔ Ballineddan. ➔ Slievemaan (see also route 27). A gate just north of a road junction leads to scenic open country which improves as one approaches the summit. (2.75 hours up, 1.5 hours down.)

10. Camarahill (GR 984929) (see also route 29). The easiest approach navigationally and one of the easiest physically, with gradually expanding views, best towards the summit. (2.5 hours up, 1.5 hours down.)

11. Knickeen (GR 983948) ➔ Army Route to Pass at GR 0296-Camenabologue (see also route 29). Forest track followed by not over-exciting country to the pass, then a lovely high level route. (4.25 hours up, 2.5 hours down.)

A WEEK IN THE MOUNTAINS

Day 1: Take the bus to Blessington. Walk to Carrig (GR 9912), climb Lugnagun, Sorrel, Black Hill, descend to Ballyknockan. Overnight in Ballyknockan. (See also route 23.)

Day 2: Climb Round Hill, Table, Lobawn, descend to Ballinclea youth hostel. Overnight in the hostel. (See also routes 26, 28.)

Day 3: Climb Camarahill, Lugnaquillia, Slievemaan. Overnight in Aghavannagh youth hostel. (See also routes 20, 29.)

Day 4: Climb Croaghanmoira, Fananierin, climb to the col west of Mullacor, descend Spink to Glendalough youth hostel. (See also routes 15, 18.)

Day 5: Free day in Glendalough.

Day 6: Climb Scarr, walk Cloghoge valley, climb to Pier Gates (GR 1706). Overnight in Roundwood area. (See also routes 8, 16.)

Day 7: Climb southern spur of Djouce, Djouce, War Hill, Tonduffs, descend to Crone carpark. Walk to Enniskerry for bus or overnight in Knockree youth hostel. (See also routes 5, 9, 10.)